THE TRUTH

ABOUT

THE HARBINGER

THE TRUTH
ABOUT
THE HARBINGER

JOSE BERNAL

CHARISMA
HOUSE

Most CHARISMA HOUSE BOOK GROUP products are available at special quantity discounts for bulk purchase for sales promotions, premiums, fund-raising, and educational needs. For details, write Charisma House Book Group, 600 Rinehart Road, Lake Mary, Florida 32746, or telephone (407) 333-0600.

THE TRUTH ABOUT *THE HARBINGER*
    by Jose Bernal
Published by Charisma House
Charisma Media/Charisma House Book Group
600 Rinehart Road
Lake Mary, Florida 32746
www.charismahouse.com

Unless otherwise noted, all Scripture quotations are from the New American Standard Bible. Copyright © 1960, 1962, 1963, 1968, 1971, 1972, 1973, 1975, 1977, 1995 by the Lockman Foundation. Used by permission. (www.Lockman.org)

Scripture quotations marked NKJV are from the New King James Version of the Bible. Copyright © 1979, 1980, 1982 by Thomas Nelson, Inc., publishers. Used by permission.

Cover design by Justin Evans
Design Director: Bill Johnson

Visit the author's website at
www.avoiceincyberspace.blogspot.com,
The Pepster's Post: A Voice in Cyber Space.

Library of Congress Cataloging-in-Publication
Data:
An application to register this book for
cataloging has been submitted to the Library of
Congress.
International Standard Book Number:
978-1-62136-569-3
E-book ISBN: 978-1-62136-570-9

While the author has made every effort to
provide accurate telephone numbers and
Internet addresses at the time of publication,
neither the publisher nor the author assumes
any responsibility for errors or for changes that
occur after publication.

The names of all critics were intentionally left
out in an effort to keep the discussion focused
on the ideas being expressed rather than being a
personal attack on anyone.

First edition

13 14 15 16 17 — 987654321
Printed in the United States of America

Contents

SECTION I

AN OVERVIEW OF *THE HARBINGER* AND WHAT'S BEING SAID ABOUT IT

Chapter 1

The PHENOMENON of
THE HARBINGER

Wʜᴇɴ *Tʜᴇ Hᴀʀʙɪɴɢᴇʀ* first hit the bookstores in the early part of 2012, very few—if any—had any idea what this small book would become and how it would impact countless numbers of people across the country.

From the first moments after it released, it appeared—and still is, at the time of this writing—on the *New York Times* best-seller list, a truly remarkable feat, given that the list is secular. Immediately upon release, the book began to change people's lives with its message.

The Harbinger has been hailed by religious and secular leaders alike, from Mike Huckabee to Michele Bachmann, from Pat Boone to Pat Robertson. It has transcended denominational borders, being praised by Baptist and charismatic leaders. It has been read by Orthodox Jews, Catholics, Mormons, the skeptical, the irreligious, and the atheist. It has been studied and taught in the halls of theological seminaries and churches. It has been spread through the halls of Congress.

Words used to describe it range from *amazing* to *stunning* to *mind-blowing* to *the most important book to come out in years*.

Its author, Jonathan Cahn, has become a fixture on television and radio shows. He has left some of the most famous interviewers stunned and speechless—and one literally bent over from amazement.

The Harbinger has triggered movements of prayer, repentance, and revival. It has initiated more than one gathering in the nation's capital and a national day of prayer. It has led more than one media personality to urgently implore the audience, "You *must* get this book!"

Wherever its message has been shared, the result has been amazement. Its accompanying volume, *The Harbinger Companion With Study Guide*, has also become a best seller. Whenever its message has been converted to other forms of media, the result has been the same: it becomes a phenomenon and breaks records.

The Harbinger has also changed multitudes of lives. Testimonies abound of people changed, of lives radically altered for God, of salvation, of repentance, and of revival, both individually and corporately.

"The Most Amazing Book I Have Ever Read!"

Below are some of the comments posted by readers on the Web that are typical reactions to *The Harbinger*:

> I believe this is the most important book written in this century, and possibly ever!…I finished the book saying, "I am blown away!"

Other than the scriptures, this is THE most amazing book that I have ever read! I could not set it down. Everyone who I know who has also read this book has had a similar response.

You will be spellbound.

It's rare that I would read a book more than once but this book leaves me speechless.

It will rock your world.

This book was totally amazing, It blew my mind over and over again.... This book will really have you saying Oh My God!!

Best book I ever read in my life!

Every American should read this book!!!!!!!

I started reading it and could not put it down. It was like a magnet pulling me to it until I had finished reading it. This book is riveting.

I tell every single person I speak to, to read this book, NOW! It has already changed so many lives.

All I can say is WOW!

And here is what Terry James of *Rapture Ready* says:

A phenomenon has taken place in the book publishing world. The secular book market—headed by the *New York Times* best-sellers list—has let slip through its normally anti-Christian critics' hands a book of profound significance. It is on the surface a work of fiction that is at the same time deeply ingrained truth from the only source of truth there is—the very Word of God.

Not since Hal Lindsey's *Late, Great Planet Earth* and Tim LaHaye and Jerry Jenkins' Left Behind series has such a volume been allowed to reach such a mass audience by those who control that level of mega sales in the book publishing industry....

I've been studying Bible prophecy for more than fifty years....In all that time, I haven't seen a case for current issues and events as having prophetic relevance presented in a more evidence-based way than in this book....

It is obvious. The Lord of Heaven wanted this book written and disseminated widely.[1]

The Harbinger Has Even Entered the Halls of Congress

The publication of *The Harbinger* has opened doors for the message of the gospel to reach places and people who otherwise would not be reached. It has now reached the nation's government, and it is breaking through partisan political and religious barriers. These are but a very few examples.

On Monday, January 21, 2013, as Barack Obama was being sworn in for a second term in Washington DC, a group of the nation's evangelical leaders from across the theological spectrum gathered in our nation's capital and held an Inaugural Prayer Breakfast, a holy convocation to the Lord for the nation.

At the breakfast, many religious leaders spoke, and one of them was pastor and Messianic rabbi Jonathan Cahn. His message was a challenge to the nation to turn to God and seek Him with all of their hearts. Before he was finished addressing those gathered, Pastor Cahn directed his next words to the president of the United States with this challenge:

> Mr. President, we come here to pray for America, for its government, for you, its leader, and for its future. We pray for your blessing and your prosperity in the will of God, because only in the will of God can we know true blessing.
>
> The answer is not found in the agendas of man or political parties, but the answer is found in that object upon which your hand will rest, upon the Word of God. For everything else will pass away, but the Word of God will abide forever.
>
> So, it must be asked in respect: Can you lay your left hand upon His Word, the Word of God, and then with your right hand enact any law that would go against it?
>
> Can you invoke the name of God to assume the presidency and then in any way endorse anything which clearly wars against the ways of God that you invoke?
>
> Can you stand in the city named after our first president and perform the act that he first performed on that first day and ignore the warning he gave that day to this nation?
>
> Can you do all that and disregard the eternal rules and order of right, which heaven itself has ordained? Can you utter the words "So help me, God" if you should in any way take part in leading a nation farther from God that you invoke to help? We pray for your blessing in the will of God.
>
> For if a nation that once knew the Almighty is called to return to Him, then so, too, must the one who leads it. You will hold in your hand the Bible of Abraham Lincoln. But do you not

know what Lincoln said and did in the midst of
the darkness that engulfed this land once before,
the darkness he saw as the righteous judgment
of God?

Lincoln issued a call to the nation. He said
this:

> It is the duty of nations as well as of men
> to own their dependence on the overruling
> power of God. To confess their sins and
> transgressions in humble sorrow with the
> assured hope that genuine repentance will
> lead to mercy and pardon and to recognize
> the sublime truth announced in the Holy
> Scriptures and proven by all history that
> those nations are only blessed whose God
> is the Lord.
>
> And, insomuch as we know that by
> His divine law, nations, like individuals,
> are subjected to punishments and
> chastisements in this world, may we not
> justly fear that this awful calamity of civil
> war which now desolates the land may be
> but punishment inflicted upon it, upon
> us, for our own presumptuous sins to the
> needful end of our national reformation as
> a whole people?
>
> We have forgotten God. We have
> forgotten the gracious hand that preserved
> us in peace and multiplied it and enriched
> and strengthened us. It behooves us then,
> to humble ourselves before the offended
> power; to confess our national sins and to
> pray for clemency and forgiveness.

So, Lincoln set forth this call to America to repent, to turn to God, to seek His mercy, and soon after that call went forth, the tide of war began to turn that would ultimately lead to national healing.

The words of Abraham Lincoln ring out to us today that those nations only are blessed whose God is the Lord. Has this nation grown so far from God that we cannot even imagine a president doing so today? Mr. President, if you seek— if you look to Lincoln as your model, then dare to follow him in his actions.[2]

This was an amazing speech, based primarily upon *The Harbinger*, culminating with the following call to turn to God for salvation:

The shadow of judgment is upon us, and for those who would ask, "How, in light of judgment, can one be saved or safe?" we give the answer: The word in Hebrew for safety and salvation is *Yeshua*. *Yeshua* is the name which we know in English as *Jesus*.

Outside of Him, there is no safety. But inside of Him, there is no fear. It was for Him and in His name that this nation, this civilization, this city on the hill named America came into existence. And it's only in Him and in His name that its problems can ultimately be answered. He remains the answer, the light in the darkness, the hope when all other hopes are faded and gone.[3]

Then, on Wednesday, May 8, 2013, Jonathan Cahn spoke at a special gathering for various members of Congress. Among the speakers were Newt Gingrich and Michele Bachmann. Even former members of Congress were in attendance, such as J. C. Watts, an ordained minister.

The gathering took place on Capitol Hill, inside the Capitol Building in Statuary Hall, the meeting place of the original House of Representatives (next to the present one). This event, we are told, was actually birthed because of *The Harbinger*.

Members of Congress have read the book, and reports have been coming that it has reached across party lines and has led many of our elected officials to gather for prayer for this nation. This is an amazing thing!

A Prophetic Word to America

The phenomenon of *The Harbinger* and its impact on America has not run its course; it has not finished but has only begun to be felt across the nation. What we are witnessing are the signs of a tide-turning event—what may be a watershed, if you will—since repentance begins with a nation's leaders and with its people.

When Jonah preached a message of impending judgment to a Gentile nation, it was received by its leaders and its people, and though there was no promise of forgiveness in it, the leaders and the people repented, and God withheld His wrath from that generation.

The message of *The Harbinger* promises hope, for in it there is the hope of forgiveness, reconciliation, salvation, redemption, restoration, and recovery. But the message must be heeded and acted upon in order for God's wrath to be averted and our nation restored.

Today is the day to act upon this message. Now is the hour of salvation. The time is short, but *The Harbinger* is reaching even the unreachable, and we are beginning to see the tide turn. It is turning very slowly in some places, but in others it is like a flood. The lives that have turned to God are the living testimonies of a work of God that may be His catalyst to call this great nation, founded as a beacon of liberty and freedom, to once again be as a city on a hill shining brightly for the Lord.

Stories like these are being heard across the nation. But if only a single person is brought in repentance to Jesus, it will have accomplished its mission, because one by one, we must all stand before the God of heaven and give an account to Him for our lives and how we have lived them.

This is the purpose of the gospel—to bring souls to repentance and to lead them to redemption in Jesus and the salvation of their souls. It begins with each person in America, until the entire nation makes peace with its Maker. Then America can be spared impending judgment, just as God told Abraham about Sodom and Gomorrah that He would spare the city if even one righteous person dwelled in it.

Chapter 2

The MYSTERY,
the MESSAGE,
and the WARNING

JONATHAN CAHN'S *THE Harbinger* unveils a two-and-a-half-thousand-year-old mystery that provides the reader with a biblical foundation for understanding what is happening in the twenty-first century—from politics to the economy to foreign affairs.

In an article written to answer some of his critics, Jonathan Cahn gives this brief overview of the book:

> *The Harbinger* concerns an ancient pattern of judgment that manifested in the last days of ancient Israel and which is now manifesting in America. What has stunned or amazed most readers is how specifically, exactly, precisely this pattern has manifested on American soil—thus the subtitle: "The ancient mystery that holds the secret of America's future." It's a mystery that lies behind everything from 9/11, to the War on Terror, to crashing of Wall Street and the collapse of the American economy, to the Great Recession. The mystery is so precise that it involves exact events, the exact actions and words of American leaders, and the exact dates of the greatest financial crashes in American

history. It is prophetic in nature in that it is a call to the nation, to the saved and the unsaved and, I have no doubt, meant for such a time as this. It concerns every American and, in a more general sense, the world, and the age. Nor do I have any doubt that the message is a wake-up call, an alarm that is both urgent and critical.[1]

In this chapter we will briefly highlight that mystery and review the nine harbingers of warning that frame the message of *The Harbinger* and this biblical mystery. These warnings will provide the readers of this book with a biblical pattern—a template—revealing God's promise for Israel and His promise for America if we heed the warning and apply the biblical pattern to our lives today.

> The bricks have fallen down,
> But we will rebuild with hewn stones;
> The sycamores are cut down,
> But we will replace them with cedars.
>   —ISAIAH 9:10, NKJV

We begin with a backward look at the nine harbingers of warning contained in the mystery of Isaiah 9:10.

The First Harbinger: The Breach

God removed His hedge of protection from Israel, resulting in Assyria's invasion in 732 BC. For America, the proof that God had removed His hedge of divine protection around this nation came with the terrorist attacks on September 11, 2001.

On the morning of Tuesday, September 11, 2001, America's first shaking took place. The

breach was established at Ground Zero when
Flight 11 struck the World Trade Center's North
Tower and Flight 175 struck the South Tower.
Flight 77 crashed into the Pentagon in Wash-
ington DC, and Flight 93, said to be headed
for the White House, crashed in Shanksville,
Pennsylvania.

This first warning went unheeded, and the
nation continued to degenerate morally. In fact,
since 9/11, America's spiritual, moral, economic,
and military decline has accelerated unabated.

The Second Harbinger: The Terrorist

For Israel, the Assyrians acted like modern-day
terrorists. The Assyrians used terror to conquer
the nations in the region of the Middle East. For
America, the terrorists of 9/11, who were from the
same region, acted using terror as a method to
attack their prey.

The tactics of the ancient Assyrians were
extremely severe: "Their punishments included
dismemberment (cutting off limbs, ears, nose, lips,
castration, etc.), impalement upon a stake, and
forced hard labor for their captives. In rebellious
cities, prisoners of war were flayed (skinned) alive,
blinded, or had their tongues torn out; they were
impaled, burned, and put to death in other ways."[2]

Modern terrorists use the same tactics as
those of the ancient Assyrians. They speak a language similar to that spoken by the Assyrians,
and they come from the same region of the world.
They are the spiritual children of these Assyrians
in every way.

The Third Harbinger: The Fallen Bricks

The inferior construction of the clay bricks of Israel's eighth-century BC walls fell to the ground after the Assyrian attack. These fallen bricks stand as a metaphor for the destruction that took place at 9/11 and the fallen twin towers.

In much the same manner, the Israelites' defiant declaration that they would rebuild their nation with stronger, better materials is also a parallel of America's same defiant determination following its first shaking to replace the debris at Ground Zero with an edifice constructed of stronger material than previously used, one that would stand higher than the towers that once stood on that hallowed ground.

The Fourth Harbinger: The Tower

Israel's leaders in the eighth century BC defied God by rebuilding the city without any evidence of repentance. America's leaders defied God by planning to replace the twin towers that were destroyed on 9/11 without any sign of national repentance, either from its leaders or from its citizens. A short period of mourning occurred, during which people flocked to houses of worship, but that period was not followed by repentance, revival, or a seeking after God. The nation, in fact, degenerated further and has continued this trend since. The leaders would replace the twin towers with the Freedom Tower, which is now called One World Trade Center.

Man's efforts to erect a world system without

God and in defiance of Him has always been
doomed to failure. It is interesting to note that
the Septuagint's Greek translation of the Bible
(also known as "LXX") renders Isaiah 9:8–10 as
follows:

> The Lord has sent death upon Jacob, and it has
> come upon Israel. And all the people of Ephraim,
> and they that dwelt in Samaria shall know, who
> say in their pride and lofty heart, The bricks are
> fallen down, but come, let us hew stones, and cut
> down sycamores and cedars, and let us build for
> ourselves a tower.

The LXX predates the modern Masoretic text
by approximately one thousand years and was
widely used by the writers of the New Testament,
who also used the Greek language because they
wrote mostly to Gentiles and because it was the
lingua franca in the conquered territories of the
Roman Empire in their day.

The Fifth Harbinger: The Gazit Stone

In the eighth century, Israel used quarried and
dressed stones to rebuild, rather than clay bricks.
For America, a quarried and dressed Adirondack
stone was the cornerstone of the new Freedom
Tower at the 9/11 site of Ground Zero. Adirondack granite, a parallel to the biblical Gazit Stone
(which meant "quarried, polished"), was lowered
at Ground Zero for the new Freedom Tower. It
was called the Freedom Stone.

New York Governor George Pataki presided
over the ceremony with the following words:

"Today is indeed a momentous day. Today we take twenty tons of Adirondack granite—the bedrock of our State—and place it as the foundation, the bedrock, of this new symbol of American strength and confidence. Today, we lay the cornerstone for a new symbol of this City and this country, and of our resolve to triumph in the face [of] terror. Today we build the Freedom Tower."[3]

The Sixth Harbinger: The Sycamore

The Middle Eastern sycamore, North American sycamore, and British sycamore trees shed their leaves in the fall and regrow them in the spring. The sycamore tree, also known as the mulberry tree, is known in Hebrew as *shakam*, and its Greek equivalent is *sukos*. For the mulberry, it is *moros* or *sukamoros*.

Most of Israel's fig-mulberry (sycamore) trees were cut down by the invading Assyrians. In America, a lone American sycamore stood in the yard of St. Paul's Chapel near the World Trade Center. It was uprooted and knocked down as it shielded the chapel from the falling debris when the towers collapsed on 9/11.

This chapel is where the new nation of the United States was first consecrated to God on April 30, 1789, by its newly inaugurated president in the first joint session of Congress. The consecration of the United States in the chapel was its first act.[4]

The fallen sycamore tree is a sign of uprooting—the uprooting of a kingdom or a nation. The falling debris from the twin towers struck and uprooted

a tree on a plot of ground on the corner of Ground
Zero. This tree became a symbol of 9/11, and it
was a sycamore tree.

The Seventh Harbinger: The Erez Tree

In the eighth century, Israel intended to replace
the destroyed sycamore with cedar trees, in defiance of God. In America, a Norway spruce was
planted at Ground Zero as an act of national
pride and defiance against the devastation following the terrorist's first strike and God's first
warning.[5]

At 4:00 p.m. on Saturday, November 29, 2003,
marking Thanksgiving and the beginning of the
holiday season, the inaugural lighting of the "Tree
of Hope"—a twenty-one-foot Norway spruce—
took place in the northwest corner of the chapel's churchyard, across the street from the World
Trade Center site. It replaced the sycamore tree
that was destroyed on September 11, 2001, by
debris from the collapsing towers.

The Eighth Harbinger: The Utterance

Words of defiant pride and arrogance were uttered
by Israel after Assyria's invasion in 732 BC. In
America, when its leaders repeated Isaiah 9:10,
they unknowingly set the stage for America's vow
to defy God's judgment on America.

On September 11, 2004, before the Congressional Black Caucus, Senator John Edwards also
quoted Isaiah 9:10.[6] This elected official represented the highest branch of the upper chamber of

our government, the US Senate, when he declared the ancient vow by quoting Isaiah 9:10.

The Ninth Harbinger: The Prophecy

For Israel, in 732 BC, Isaiah 9:10 followed a pattern of prophetic pronouncement of judgment from God for what would happen to Israel ten years later, in 722 BC. For America, Isaiah 9:10 likewise follows the same pattern of a pronouncement of judgment from God through the utterance of that scripture by America's leaders following the events of 9/11.

The biblical prophetic pattern is recurring, with September 11, 2001, as its commencement. On September 12, 2001, Senate Majority Leader Tom Daschle quoted Isaiah 9:10 in a speech before the US Senate on Capitol Hill, and he added, with resolve and defiance, "This is what we will do. We will rebuild and we will recover."[7] The connection made by two of America's highest elected officials—Daschle and Edwards—each citing the prophecy of Isaiah 9:10 and applying it directly to the tragic events of 9/11, set the harbingers into motion. As it was for ancient Israel a warning, so it would be for America.

The Isaiah 9:10 Effect

The initial warning God gave ancient Israel was ignored and rejected. As a result, it suffered a second shaking, where its attempts at restoration failed. So too has it happened with America. Rather than listen to God's warning, the nation became more brazen. Once again God would shake America to bring about repentance in order to avert judgment.

This came in the form of the Great Recession. September 11 was followed precisely seven years later with the meltdown of Wall Street and the greatest economic collapse since the Great Depression.[8] The words spoken by America's leaders following September 11 triggered the Isaiah 9:10 Effect, which witnessed the real-estate collapse and the meltdown on Wall Street seven years later. We are also now seeing the diminished power of American military might as the armed forces are reduced due to sequestering.

The Uprooted

God planted Israel, but He uprooted its people from the land because they broke His covenant with them and refused to listen to the warnings of His prophets. Instead, they listened to the assurances of their false prophets, who promised them safety and false security. Because of this, God brought a second shaking to ancient Israel when the Assyrians invaded ten years later, carrying the northern tribes of Manasseh and Ephraim away in exile.[9]

The same pattern was witnessed after 9/11 in America in the same order described in Isaiah 9:10. Because there was no repentance and America's leaders increasingly left God out of the picture and banned the reading of His Word or prayer in Jesus' name from public gatherings, every effort of theirs to recover was bound to fail. Judgment loomed. First comes the breaking down—the fallen bricks. Then comes the uprooting—the sycamore.

The lone sycamore tree that stood in the yard of St. Paul's Chapel near the World Trade Center, which was uprooted and knocked down as it shielded the chapel from the falling debris when the towers collapsed on 9/11, symbolized the second shaking in America. The words spoken at the planting of the new tree were, "This Ground Zero Tree of Hope will be a sign of the indomitable nature of human hope."[10] *Indomitable* means "unconquerable."

Thus, the two images of national judgment presented themselves in America—and in the same order. The first shaking was the fallen towers, and the second shaking was the uprooting of the tree.

The Mystery of the Shemitah

In the Mosaic Law, it was required that every seventh year Israel had to allow the land to completely rest, with no harvesting, reaping, or any other work being done in the fields. Additionally, all debts were to be canceled (Deut. 15:1–2). This was called the *Shemitah*.[11]

When Israel broke the Mosaic Law, it broke the covenant that established that Law and therefore invoked God's judgment on the nation. Since Israel did not allow for the Shemitah, but rebelled and did not keep the Sabbath year, God imposed it on them through invasions.

Like it was for ancient Israel, the key that holds the timing of America's judgment is hidden in the mystery of the Shemitah. This Shemitah came to pass for America on September 29, 2008, precisely seven years after the events of September 11, 2001, with the stock market suffering its worst crash in history as the Dow Jones Industrial Average fell 777 points.

America was plunged into the Great Recession, the greatest economic collapse since the Great Depression—even worse than the Carter recession of the 1970s—and America has not yet emerged from it. Instead, the recession has gone globally viral, affecting the economies of Europe, Asia, and the other Western nations.

When did the crash occur? In the Hebrew month of Elul. On what day? The twenty-ninth day of Elul. Elul 29 of that year was not just any day, but the end of the seven-year lunar cycle of years known as the Shemitah.

The Third Witness

Senate Majority Leader Tom Daschle's remarks to the joint session of Congress on September 12, 2001, in which he quoted Isaiah 9:10 and then said, "That is what we will do. We will rebuild"—this was the first witness.

The second witness was Senator John Edwards, when he gave his speech to the Congressional Black Caucus and framed his entire address around the ancient vow quoted in Isaiah 9:10.

The third witness was President Barack Obama, who in his first State of the Union address on February 24, 2009, framed his speech around the theme "We will rebuild. We will recover." This paraphrased the ancient vow, and he prefaced it by saying, "I want every American to know this: We will rebuild. We will recover."[12]

The declaration made by President Obama to rebuild and recover did not acknowledge God's grace but was instead declared in the same self-will cited directly in Isaiah's prophecy. In this first speech to Congress, President Obama was the third person to speak this defiant vow without acknowledging God.

According to Mosaic Law, three witnesses are needed to establish a matter—any matter. In the case of America, the citing of Isaiah 9:10 by these three witnesses connects the prophecy to the nation's resolve to rebuild, replant, and recover and sets in motion a biblical, legal precedent over its fate: imminent judgment.

The Mystery Ground

The United States of America was consecrated by prayer to God on the corner of what would become Ground Zero. It was there all of the nation's new leaders gathered—all of the Founding Fathers— and it was there God's hedge of protection spread over the land at its founding on April 30, 1789. It was there where its hedge of protection was also lifted on September 11, 2001. The nation's ground of consecration became its ground of judgment— its uprooting—when its hedge of protection was lifted on 9/11.

It was there, at the corner of Ground Zero, that the towers collapsed. It was there that the founders gathered to commit the future of this

nation to God's holy protection, and it was there
that this holy protection was removed.[13]

Things to Come

Where does America fit in prophecy? The Bible
is silent about this, but there is a reason why. It
lies in the hope that God's people will heed the
call of God at this hour and turn this nation and
its leaders back to the only One who can avert its
judgment—almighty God.

In his remarks at the Presidential Inaugural
Prayer Breakfast, Jonathan Cahn said the
following:

> How does judgment come to a nation? After
> defying all of God's calls and warnings, the nation
> of Israel would experience something unprece-
> dented. It was the opening stage of judgment. God
> removed one of Israel's blessings. Years before the
> nation's destruction, He allowed its hedge of pro-
> tection to be lifted. He allowed an enemy to make
> a strike on the land. It was a wake-up call to avert
> national destruction.[14]

Israel forgot God, and now we too have forgotten. A spiritual amnesia has overtaken America.
America has forgotten her God. So it came to pass
that in America on September 11, 2001, its hedge
of protection was lifted. An enemy was allowed to
make a strike on the land. It was temporary and
contained. It was a wake-up call. We all sensed it,
even if we didn't say it. As Jonathan Cahn put it:

> And for a short time it looked as if America
> would wake up…as if we were on the verge of

a national revival. People flocked to churches and spoke of God. And then, a few weeks later, it was all over. There was no revival. There was no change of course. America continued down its course of spiritual departure from God but did so now with even more fervor. Eleven years after 9/11, the nation stands not closer to God, but much farther away.[15]

But there is hope yet for America, for the Lord has promised, "If I shut up the heavens so that there is no rain, or if I command the locust to devour the land, or if I send pestilence among My people, and My people who are called by My name humble themselves and pray and seek My face and turn from their wicked ways, then I will hear from heaven, will forgive their sin and will heal their land" (2 Chron. 7:13–14).

The smiles of heaven cannot remain on a nation that disregards the ways of God. If America continues spiraling away from God, its blessings will likewise be removed and replaced with judgment. But if it repents and turns to God, it will experience a national revival, the likes of which has never been witnessed before in its history, and the blessings of almighty God will once again be bestowed on the nation and its people.

But God's people must turn to God. Who are God's people? We are His people—the ones who have made peace with God through the Messiah Jesus, Jews and Gentiles all across this great nation who call on His name for our redemption and must now call on His name for His mercy for our nation.

Eternity

"And what will you do on the Day of Judgment?"

Would you want everyone to know, to turn to God, to accept Jesus as their own personal Savior and be saved?

Would you tell them? Warn them?

Judgment is not a matter of geography; it is a matter of where you are personally with God. Are you ready to meet Him?

Have you given thought to your eternal destiny once you break the bonds of this life and stand before His presence to account for yourself?

The Scripture warns, "And inasmuch as it is appointed for men to die once and after this comes judgment" (Heb. 9:27). But take note of the following scriptural promise to all who call upon the name of Jesus: "So Christ also, having been offered once to bear the sins of many, will appear a second time for salvation without reference to sin, to those who eagerly await Him" (v. 28).

The Last Seal

Nouriel Kaplan describes the last seal to Anna Goren in the story this way:

> The writing on the seal was in a language I had never seen before. But I remembered the words of the prophet that day we first met on the bench, when he took the seal to examine it. He said it was Hebrew, but a different form of Hebrew— Paleo-Hebrew, an older version.[16]

In *The Harbinger*, the seal of Baruch leads Nouriel on a journey of nine seals, a journey that ends with his writing a book. In reality, it was the seal of Baruch that led Jonathan Cahn to write of the nine seals in *The Harbinger*.[19]

Laying the Foundation

The Harbinger reinforces the Word of God, and through the Word and the Holy Spirit, it draws the inspiration to warn America of imminent judgment as it describes the same pattern of behavior in America that was exhibited in ancient Israel twenty-seven hundred years ago.

The purpose of *The Harbinger* is that we might heed this warning and avert judgment by seeking God through repentance, calling on Jesus to save us and spare our nation. To this end, it speaks to this generation a message it must heed and take action upon.

Chapter 3

The HARBINGERS:
ALIVE and WELL (PART 1)

Now that we've summarized the central components of *The Harbinger*, let's address what a key critic has said in an attempt to explain away the significance of the nine harbingers.

Attacking the Breach

The critic contends that the breach of 9/11 isn't really that significant since there have been other times in American history when far more were killed. Furthermore, he brings Pearl Harbor into the picture. America was attacked then, as well. So why isn't Pearl Harbor significant? The charge is that because Pearl Harbor and other times when more Americans lost their lives aren't given any significance as harbingers, we can dismiss 9/11 as having the significance of a harbinger.

The first problem with this argument is the attempt to make the warning of judgment dependent on numbers. That argument is unbiblical. One of the most famous and archetypical judgments in the Bible is that which fell on those who worshipped the golden calf. That event was more than a warning—it was an actual judgment. And how many people were killed in that judgment?

The Scripture records about three thousand people. Three thousand people is not only a number that can indicate a warning of judgment, but also the very number given in the Bible in one of the most memorable of judgments in Scripture.

9/11, Pearl Harbor, and the War of 1812

So, what about Pearl Harbor? The argument here would fall in the category of a straw man. *The Harbinger* has never presented a scenario in which any calamity or all calamities signify judgment.

The idea that 9/11 is not significant because of events such as Pearl Harbor does not hold up. There are very major and intrinsic differences between the two. Pearl Harbor took place on a military base in the Pacific. The island of Hawaii is over two thousand miles away from the continental United States. Beyond that, it wasn't even one of the states at the time. In contrast, two out of three of the plane crash sites on 9/11 took place at the heart of American culture and civilization—in the midst of New York City and in the nation's capital, Washington DC.

To find something even remotely comparable, one would have to go back almost two centuries to the War of 1812. And even here, the dynamics were completely different. The War of 1812 was declared by the United States. The British response was to attack Washington. The United States emerged from that war with a sense of euphoric victory, not to mention a national anthem. Even if one includes the War of 1812 in the analysis, 9/11 would have been the first such strike or breach of the American continent in almost two centuries.

The Era of Good Feelings and Global Superpower

It's true that 9/11 remains the only such strike on the American continent in modern history and one that left a crippling blow on American culture and consciousness. The War of 1812 actually resulted in what was called the "Era of Good Feelings." And Pearl Harbor was a central component of America's rise to become the world's preeminent and unquestioned financial, economic, and military superpower. The attack on 9/11, on the other hand, has led to no such thing, neither an "Era of Good Feelings" nor an extraordinary rise to world power. Rather, it has led, more than anything, to an increased foreboding concerning America's future and increasing signs of the decline of American civilization.

Further, none of the previous events came at a time when American culture had descended so deeply into moral decline and spiritual apostasy—or become so diametrically opposed to the faith and morality of Scripture. Only in this context can the harbingers and the ancient progression exist. This was only true in the latter case—9/11.

Roosevelt and the Missing Harbingers

To even bring an event like Pearl Harbor into this discussion, one would have to ignore something that is simply missing—the harbingers. Pearl Harbor possesses no connection to the harbingers or, for that matter, to a clear and precise biblical template of judgment. There is no symbolic or archetypical sycamore to be struck down. There is no act of *khalaf*, the ritual replacing of the one tree with another, no *erez* tree, no utterance of the ancient vow of judgment, which also links up with all the other manifestations of harbingers. To even begin comparing the two, instead of declaring December 7 to be a date which would "live in infamy," Franklin Delano Roosevelt would have had to proclaim the ancient vow of Isaiah 9:10. It never happened. There were no harbingers and no connections. But in the case of 9/11, the connections are clearly there, and they are there over and over again.

The critic makes another charge. He says that just because there was an attack on America on September 11, that doesn't mean God allowed America's hedge of protection to be lifted. This has to be one of the strangest of arguments. America was attacked. That means its protection was breached. This attack was clearly allowed by the hand of God.

The only thing left to argue would be the difference between God removing the hedge of protection and God allowing the hedge of protection to be removed. But we might as well argue how many angels can dance on the head of a needle. We'll pass on that.

Attacking the Assyrians

The critic charges that one cannot link the terrorists of 9/11 to the ancient Assyrians. He bases this on the fact that one cannot say the terrorists were the flesh-and-blood descendants of the ancient Assyrians.

Again, it's a straw-man argument. The connection in *The Harbinger* between al Qaeda and the ancient Assyrians is not in any way dependent on flesh and blood. The possibility that the blood of the ancient Assyrians could be flowing in the veins of those linked to 9/11 is mentioned and remains a distinct possibility, but it is not now nor has it ever been the connecting principle behind the second harbinger.

Rather, the connection is this: The attack on the land—the breach of the nation's security—is accomplished specifically by agents of terror. The Assyrians were the agents of terror in the ancient world and in the ancient case of Israel. Those who carried out the destruction of 9/11, the members of al Qaeda, are the agents of terror in the modern world and in the case of America. Added to that, the Assyrians were and still are recognized by historians as the inventors—the fathers—of terrorism. Thus, any modern-day terrorist is their historical and functional disciple.

It still remains that the Assyrians were children of the Middle East. So too were the terrorists of 9/11. The Assyrians carried out their terrorist strike in Akkadian; the terrorists of 9/11 carried out their attack in Arabic, the closest sister language to the ancient Assyrians' language still existent in the modern world. After the attack, ancient Israel was brought into contact with Assyria;

America, after its attack, was brought into conflict with Iraq, which is modern-day Assyria.

The attempted negating of the second harbinger, as with the others, falls under the category of hairsplitting on a day of judgment. The only way to satisfy such criticism would be to have had ancient Assyrians land in New York and attack the World Trade Center with bows and arrows.

Attacking the Bricks

The critic attempts an attack on the third harbinger, the fallen bricks. The argument is this: The destruction involved in 9/11 was limited; therefore, it can't be a harbinger of judgment. Further, the buildings of ancient Israel were built of clay bricks, but the buildings of New York City are built of steel and concrete. Therefore, we can dismiss any idea that 9/11 has any link to such a biblical warning.

The first error in this argument is, again, confusing scale with nature. In other words, it's the error that says there has to have been more people killed for it to have anything to do with judgment. In this case, the argument is that there had to be more destruction to constitute judgment or warning. It would be interesting to find out where such critics get their rules. Their criticisms strike many as reminiscent of the strategy of the Pharisees, who not only split hairs, strained at gnats, and swallowed camels, but also introduced all sorts of man-made rules that ended up nullifying the Word of God.

In short, no such rulebook exists. The Bible

gives no building code or destruction code as to how many buildings must be destroyed for something to constitute a warning of judgment. In fact, the Scriptures are replete with things like a single shattered jar as a prophetic warning of national judgment.[1] If God could send a warning to an entire nation through the clay pieces of a broken jar, He can certainly warn a nation through something massively greater than that, like 9/11.

As to the argument that the World Trade Center wasn't built out of clay bricks, according to such arguments, that means God could never biblically warn a modern nation of judgment—as there are no skyscrapers built of clay bricks. According to such arguments, for that matter, no pastor or Bible teacher could ever apply a Scripture to modern life, since the Scriptures were written in ancient times to ancient people, and we don't dress as they did, talk as they did, or live in the same kind of cities or buildings as they did—which means we couldn't take words written to them and apply them to our lives. Of course, this argument is, itself, unbiblical and nonsensical.

The buildings of ancient cities were made of clay bricks. The buildings of modern cities are made of steel and concrete. The functional connection is that the buildings of each city were destroyed and left in heaps of ruins. The fact that the ruin heaps of Ground Zero literally contained fallen bricks is extra.

Attacking the Tower

As for the fourth harbinger, the tower, the critic attacks it on the ground that Isaiah 9:10 doesn't mention the word *tower*. Therefore, the whole thing must be dismissed.

The first problem with this is that *The Harbinger* never says Isaiah 9:10 uses the word *tower* in the original Hebrew. The tower is the embodiment of what Isaiah 9:10 does specifically say—it is the embodiment of "We will rebuild," the nation's attempt and campaign at rebuilding itself to be bigger, better, and stronger than before. That was the case in ancient Israel, and that was the case in post-9/11 America, as America also attempted to rebuild itself stronger than before. The chief symbol of that rebuilding was the reconstruction of Ground Zero, the central object of which was a tower. The central point is not the existence of a tower, but rather the campaign to rebuild that which was destroyed in the attack. Were towers part of the ancient campaign to rebuild Israel? It is very likely they were. But none of this prophecy or connection is dependent on the specific embodiment of a tower.

Nevertheless, it turns out that the oldest translation of the Bible, the Greek Septuagint, when translating Isaiah 9:10, does so with the words, "The bricks are fallen. Come let us build for ourselves a *tower*" (emphasis added). So, the ancient translation actually mentions a tower. But the critic protests that one can't use the translation in the Septuagint when opening up a biblical text. Really? How about the New Testament? The New Testament uses the Septuagint version all the time, even with its peculiarities. *The Harbinger* maintains the difference between the original Hebrew and the Greek Septuagint. Nevertheless, the point is not that the Septuagint is more accurate than the Hebrew or that this was what Isaiah intended to say. The point is, again, that these are signs of warning. The tower is relevant to the Hebrew original in that it comprises the embodiment of the nation's campaign to rebuild itself. The fact that the most ancient translation of Isaiah 9:10 actually speaks of a tower is, again, not required—but thoroughly fascinating.

Attacking the Stone

The critic attempts to attack the fifth harbinger, the Gazit Stone. On what grounds? On the grounds that the people of ancient Israel used many gazit stones, while the people of New York used only one. Further, he argues, the Gazit Stone of Ground Zero was ultimately removed from the site.

As for the first point, again, we have the use of a rulebook that nobody can locate. No such stipulation exists in the Bible. In fact, it is just the opposite. In the New Testament, the Messiah, Jesus, is referred to as the Lamb of God. The designation refers to the sacrificial lambs in the temple, and specifically to lambs offered up on the Hebrew feast of Passover. The two are intrinsically linked together in Scripture.

But wait a minute. Jesus is called the Lamb of God, but there wasn't just one lamb of God— there were *many* lambs of God. In fact, there were hundreds of thousands of lambs of God. So by this logic (and this rulebook), the Messiah could not be the Lamb of God, since He is only one and the lambs of God were many. For the apostle Paul to write, "Christ our Passover also has been sacrificed" (1 Cor. 5:7), would, by such arguments, have to be a twisting of Scripture, since there were many Passover lambs spoken of in the Bible, but the Messiah is only one. Such trains of argument would nullify much biblical revelation for the central fact that they aren't biblical and cannot be applied to biblical subjects.

But this reveals a very central flaw in most of these arguments: They are mistaking a biblical pattern, or template, and the replaying of biblical principles and signs for the actual fulfillment of biblical prophecy. If we were saying Isaiah 9:10 was actually speaking about 9/11 or also speaking about America, then we could bring up such questions. But *The Harbinger* never says Isaiah 9:10 was prophesying about America, but rather Israel. No matter how many times this is clearly stated, such critics appear to just not get it, whether unintentionally or intentionally.

Rather, we are dealing with signs of judgment, warnings given to a nation, signs that follow an ancient biblical pattern and progression, and the manifestations of patterns. The question rather is, Can God use a biblical pattern and Scripture given to an ancient nation to now warn a modern one? And the answer is *absolutely yes*. As to the rules He must follow to do this, these are man-made and not from God. He is under no such obligation.

As to the removal of the Gazit Stone years later, does this, as the critic maintains, in any way negate the sign? Where is it written that the Gazit Stone must stay on that ground forever in order to have constituted a sign? Nowhere, as usual.

The fact is, the people of New York, as did the people of ancient Israel, quarried out a Gazit Stone. The fact is, the people of New York brought it back to the ground of destruction, as would have been done in the last days of ancient Israel. The fact is, this became their "stone of defiance," the beginning of their national rebuilding, a symbol of their resolve. They held a ceremony around the stone. American leaders gathered at the ceremony and focused on the stone. They pronounced vows of national defiance around the stone, even using the exact words of a phrase linked to Isaiah 9:10.

Attacking the Sycamore

As for the sixth harbinger, the sycamore, the critic seeks to nullify it on the grounds that it is not the exact Middle Eastern tree that grows in Israel.

It's hard to build an argument to attack *The Harbinger* on a fact that *The Harbinger* explicitly states from the outset. The ancient Hebrew syc-amore, the *shakam*, only grows naturally in cli-mates like that of the Middle East. It doesn't naturally grow in the American northeast, such as New York City. However, the amazing thing is that, nevertheless, on September 11, 2001, the sixth harbinger, the sign of the sycamore, was still manifested in New York City. Before its collapse, the fallen tower struck down a nearby object—a tree. What kind of tree? A sycamore.

The harbingers are signs. Signs are only signs so much as they signify something. They must, in some way, speak. They are signs appointed to speak to a specific nation. The Middle Eastern sycamore was the appropriate sign to speak to a Middle Eastern nation. The Western sycamore was the appropriate sign to speak to a Western nation. To demand that a Middle Eastern sign be employed when speaking to a Western nation would be the same as requiring American leaders to speak their words in ancient Hebrew.

Can God "translate" a sign so it matches its context? Of course. The entire New Testament is an example of that. Words, phrases, and even concepts are used in a Greek and non–Middle Eastern setting to bring biblical and Middle Eastern realities to a new people. This translation takes place on even deeper levels in Scripture. Again, we go back to the Messiah being called the Lamb of God. The concept of the sacrificial lamb was translated from a Levitical or animal context to that of the Messiah, a human being. But such critics, by their train of logic, could argue that Jesus cannot be the Lamb of God, since lambs have wool and Jesus had no wool!

It is worth repeating that the tree that fell at Ground Zero was given the name *sycamore*, after the Greek *sukos moros*, which stands for the Hebrew *shakam*. In other words, the tree that was struck down on 9/11 bore the name, even in the original languages, of the Middle Eastern tree of Isaiah 9:10.

Chapter 4

The HARBINGERS: ALIVE
and WELL (PART 2)

I N THIS CHAPTER we continue our response
to one key critic's charges against the nine
harbingers.

Attacking the Erez Tree

As for the seventh harbinger, the *erez* tree, the
critic contends that the tree planted in New York
City is not the same as in Isaiah—that it is not a
cedar and therefore can be dismissed.

In the case of the sycamore, the critic argued
against the manifestation on the grounds that it
followed after the English as opposed to the
Hebrew word. Yet in this case, he, in effect,
argues the other way around—that the seventh
harbinger follows after the Hebrew as opposed
to the English word *cedar*. Most English trans-
lations will render the phrase in Isaiah 9:10 as having to do with the cedar tree. The critic argues
that the tree must be the same as the English-
rendered *cedar*. Of course, the Hebrews didn't
speak English but Hebrew. The word for what
they planted in place of the sycamore is *erez*.

The critic argues that *erez* must then mean
what we today refer to as *cedar* and that it cannot

mean *spruce*, which is the kind of tree planted at Ground Zero in place of the sycamore.

The argument, in the case, is simply false. The Hebrew word *erez* can mean *cedar*, but it is hardly and absolutely not limited by that word. The fact is that *erez* is used in ancient texts to refer to other trees beyond that of the cedar. The fact is that *erez* is even used in the Bible to refer to trees that could not possibly be cedars. For example, it is used in Scripture to refer to trees growing in the wilderness. It appears throughout Leviticus to describe a tree that grows in the desert. Cedars don't grow in the desert.

The critic ignores or avoids what most good commentaries and Bible dictionaries clearly know and state—that the Hebrew word *erez* refers to a conifer tree, a pine tree with needles and evergreen. Most specifically, the Hebrew *erez* refers to the pinaceae family of trees. The pinaceae tree can refer to a cedar, but it can also refer to other trees—namely, the spruce, the very tree that was ceremoniously planted at the corner of Ground Zero. In other words, the people of New York literally planted an *erez* tree, the same tree referred to in Isaiah 9:10, in place of the fallen sycamore, which is the very same act described in Isaiah 9:10.

Attacking the Vows and Proclamations

What about the eighth and ninth harbingers, the vow and the prophecy? Here, the manifestations are so precise as to involve the exact same phrases and words spoken in the same context and done so by prominent national leaders. What could be the objection here?

The critic argues that this doesn't mean anything, since anyone would have used that verse. He further argues that saying an American leader could be inspired by God to say such words is to equate their words with Scripture or to call them prophets. And, lastly, that since they didn't know what they were saying and didn't mean it as it was originally intended in the Bible, and since they closed their speeches with "God Bless America," we can dismiss the fact that they just pronounced the ancient vow of judgment, Isaiah 9:10, word for word.

Speeches of judgment

First, the idea that they had no choice but to say the ancient words of judgment, since the context involved destruction, just doesn't hold up. They had complete choice to say whatever they wanted to say. They didn't have to quote from the Bible, much less any other book. And if they did quote from the Bible, there is no shortage of verses that could be quoted—namely, thirty thousand verses!

Even the Hebrew word for "build," translated in some Bibles as "rebuild," appears in over 120 verses of Scripture. If there was any truth to this attempt at nullification, then this Isaiah 9:10 verse should be quoted all the time. There is no shortage of destructive events in American history, old or modern—hurricanes, fires, tornados, floods, arson, and more—that occur several times a year.

So, if this verse is the most likely verse to quote in times of destructive events, it would have to be heard almost all the time. But it is an obscure verse and very rarely heard, even in churches and among students of the Bible.

And what is the context of the verse? The verse is about national judgment. The critic argues that what most likely happened here is that a politician, wanting to quote something in calamitous times, would naturally choose a verse like this. This only shows how ludicrous the criticism is and how it argues for the exact opposite. Politicians have speechwriters and often check every word in light of their concern for political correctness or the speech's potential to offend or be used by detractors or the press. So for any politician to use a verse that is clearly about judgment and is prefaced by words that identify the verse as having been spoken by those in pride and arrogance of heart—it is nothing short of extraordinary.

The natural and the supernatural

But the attempted argument is itself founded on a false premise—namely, that if one can find any natural causes or causation for any phenomenon, then we can dismiss its significance and it can't be of God. This is entirely unbiblical. God uses both natural and supernatural causation. Jesus rode into Jerusalem on a donkey as the fulfillment of the Messianic prophecy of Zechariah 9. Was there anything overtly supernatural about it? No. There were many donkeys in Israel, and anyone could ride them. Does that in any way nullify the significance of the event? No.

Or take, for that matter, the central event of the New Testament—the crucifixion. Was crucifixion a natural or supernatural part of the Roman Empire? It was a natural part. The events that brought Jesus to trial, to sentencing, and to execution all had natural causation—the plots of men, politics, sociology, and physics. So you had a natural and common way of death and all sorts of natural causes that could send a man to the cross. Such critics argue that it was all natural and common—therefore, it has no significance.

But does the fact that all these things came through overwhelmingly natural means in any way lessen the fact that it was the fulfillment of Messianic prophecy, even that of the suffering and death of Messiah that Isaiah foretold seven centuries earlier (Isa. 53)? No. In no way does it lessen it. God uses both natural and supernatural causation.

The unwitting vessels

What about politicians saying something prophetic? Is this possible? It is not only possible, but it also already happened. As *The Harbinger* points out, this is exactly what happened with the high priest Caiaphas.[1] He told those around him that it was necessary that one man should die so that the nation would not perish. Did Caiaphas say this of his own, or was he inspired to say it? The account reveals that he did not say this of his own. It records that he was prophesying.

This doesn't mean that Caiaphas was a prophet or that his words were equivalent to Scripture (though his words are recorded in Scripture). It means that he was led by God to say what he said. In other words, God can cause leaders to say something prophetic, even if the leader is not a prophet and may not even know, much less follow, the ways of God.

What about the argument that since the American leaders invoked a blessing at the end of their speeches, this nullifies the significance of their proclamations? Does a leader who speaks a prophetic word have to be in agreement with the prophetic meaning of those words? Does he even have to know what those words signify? Not at all. Caiaphas intended only one thing when he spoke of the death of Jesus: murder. Yet his words were prophetic, as they spoke of a man dying a sacrificial death so that others would not perish.

So, did the fact that Caiaphas was plotting murder nullify the unintentionally holy nature of his statement? Not in any way. Then, by the same token, the fact that a leader could invoke a blessing at the end of his speech, heartfelt or perfunctory, in no way nullifies the unintentional prophetic nature of his statement—whether in the case of Tom Daschle or John Edwards or others.

The match with ancient Israel applies even in this, for those who originally uttered the ancient vow did so thinking it was a good thing, a vow of hope for future blessings, national prosperity, and power. But the words carried an entirely different meaning. As recorded in Isaiah 9:8–10, the words signified pride, defiance, judgment, and destruction. The ancient leaders and others who uttered them had no idea what they were saying. Neither did the American leaders who uttered those same words after 9/11.

And this is not even to grapple with the fact that not only did American leaders utter the exact words uttered by the leaders of ancient Israel in the last days of their nation, but also that those things of which they spoke—the sycamore, the stone, the replacing of the trees—were actually coming true, manifesting in America, or would come true after the words were spoken.

Summing Up

In short, the harbingers stand. The attempts to nullify them are basically the same as those employed by enemies of the gospel in their attempts to nullify the fulfillment of Messianic prophecies by Jesus. They seek to dissect and split hairs over each point while ignoring the big and obvious picture.

For example, one critic of the gospel will argue that when Isaiah 53 foretells of the Messiah who will die for our sins, it says, "He did not open His mouth" (v. 7). They then point to a scripture where Jesus said something during His arrest and execution and conclude that therefore He can't be the Messiah.

Of course, the Scripture never says that He would *never* say anything, but rather that He would go to His death like a lamb to the slaughter, silent in the face of His executioners, as one not defending Himself. This is exactly what Jesus did. He was led to the slaughter like a lamb. The overwhelmingly striking thing is that He did not defend Himself or seek to stop His execution. He was strangely silent.

Others will split hairs over a Hebrew word, arguing that the word for *death* in one verse is plural (v. 9) and that therefore Isaiah 53 is not speaking about one person but many. What they fail to say is that this peculiarity is a Hebrew figure of speech denoting intensity. And even then, the phrase doesn't say "their deaths" but "his deaths," which, if anything, would speak of one dying the death of many.

The critics' strategy is to put the prophecies and their fulfillment under a microscope and then, through the lens of that microscope, to use any technicality, any perceived hint of difference in them to undo the overwhelming weight of evidence, consistent revelation, and testimony that proves their fulfillment. With Messianic prophecy, the overwhelming fact is one of a consistent revelation of a Messiah with all the attributes of one specific person—one born in Bethlehem, entering Jerusalem on a donkey, despised and rejected of men, arrested, falsely tried, suffering for the sins of others, pierced through, killed as a sacrifice, atoning for sin, bringing healing and redemption, becoming the light of the Gentiles, and more.

Jesus Himself was continually confronted by Pharisees who, with their hairsplitting, nitpicking strategies, sought to find fault, sin, and error in Him, and ultimately sought to nullify the evidence that He was indeed the Messiah. In doing so, they missed the forest for the trees, or rather the branches, or rather the buds. In the end, not only did they miss their awaited Messiah, but they also ignored the judgment of which they were warned—a judgment that, within a few decades, would ultimately overtake them.

So too with *The Harbinger*. The attempt is to do the same—to put each harbinger under a microscope in search of any technicality or perceived variation, and then, in the process of this micro-nitpicking, to seek to undo the overwhelming weight of evidence and consistent revelation that testifies on behalf of the harbingers.

But as with the Messianic prophecies, the harbingers hold up. The consistency of the revelation stands. The fact that each and all of the harbingers have manifested in America, that all of them link to the same event (9/11), that several of them link to the same ground, that all of them occurred through different means without any one person trying to make them happen, and that all of them were further joined together by the macro-harbinger of a proclamation made on the floor of Capitol Hill the day after the calamity—any honest and unbiased reaction to the weight of these things would be something along the lines of "Wow." And, indeed, that has been the overwhelmingly typical reaction.

One could not expect that a book and message such as *The Harbinger* would not be attacked. But after all is said and done, one fact remains: *The Harbinger* stands.

Chapter 5

OTHER MYSTERIES of
THE HARBINGER EXPLAINED

ONE CRITIC CLAIMS that *The Harbinger* departs from a biblical hermeneutic, in that Isaiah 9:10, in context, concerns Israel, not America. This claim, which he brings up several times in his critique, is based on an underlying confusion—specifically, that the book is claiming that Isaiah 9:10 is a prophecy about America. The problem is that *The Harbinger* has made no such claim. It does speak of a connection between America and Israel (not exactly a novel idea), and it does speak of a mystery from the Scriptures that has an amazing application to America. But this is light-years removed from claiming that a certain scripture is prophesying of America.

The actual connection is a very simple one—namely this: God is able to bring judgment against a nation and warn a nation of that judgment, and it is His nature to both warn and call back. He is also sovereign and able to send warnings using whatever means, consistent with His nature, that He chooses. This would most certainly include giving warnings by using the same patterns of warning and judgment as revealed in the Bible. There is nothing here that is anything less than biblical and nothing here that is other than that which has been attested to in orthodox faith throughout the ages. It is, on the contrary, the argument itself that has no biblical grounding.

Further, the reappearance of such ancient patterns of judgment revealed in a particular scripture does not in any way affect the original understanding, meaning, or interpretation of that scripture in its original context—not in any way, shape, or form. Thus, the realm of hermeneutics is not, by this, touched or affected. To miss this distinction is to make a severe error and to miss what *The Harbinger* is all about.

The Harbinger never claims that Isaiah is prophesying of America, but rather something very different—that the biblical pattern, template, and signs are now repeating themselves in stunning precision and that the scripture that concerns ancient Israel is being applied to America. Is this actually stated in the book? Absolutely. The distinction is explicitly given in the very chapter where Isaiah 9:10 is first shared:

> The prophecy, in its context, concerned ancient Israel. But as a template of judgment, as a *sign*, it now concerns America.[1]

As to the context of Isaiah 9:10, *The Harbinger* clearly identifies it with ancient Israel. In fact, it is continually applied to Israel throughout the book. In addition, the surrounding history of eighth-century Samaria is fully presented. The mere fact that the book speaks of eighth-century Israel to reveal the pattern and signs that are now repeating requires that its context be that of ancient Israel. Further, the book includes quotes from the most respected and classical of Bible commentaries.

In *The Harbinger*, the hermeneutic of Isaiah 9:10 is not taken one inch away from its historical and contextual bearings, nor from its original, proper, and traditionally understood meaning—not an inch, and not even a millimeter. The critique is groundless, based on an apparent inability to distinguish the realm of scriptural interpretation from that of scriptural application. *The Harbinger's* hermeneutics remain absolutely sound.

The Isaiah 9:10 Effect

One critic has attempted to charge *The Harbinger* with "prosperity preaching" because it states that the pronouncement of the vow led to Israel's destruction. How do they manage that charge? By saying that since words could produce such results—a firmly held belief of "word of faith" teaching, also called "word-faith" teaching—they are incorrectly linking it to "prosperity preaching." How anyone could get a prosperity message out of a book warning America of national judgment is mind-boggling.

Beyond this, one critic went a further and said that such ideas are occult. This is an example of the tendency in some "discernment ministries" to jump at the prospect of linking the most superficial of resemblances at the expense of reality. (We will discuss the importance of good discernment to a greater extent in chapter 13.)

On the contrary, the Scriptures give examples

of words and statements having momentous consequences. The vow spoken in ancient Israel in Isaiah 9:10 is one of them. The vow is followed by a "therefore," which leads to a scenario of national judgment. So, by the logic of such critics, they could charge Isaiah with believing in the occult.

Of course, it has nothing to do with that—not in the case of Israel and Isaiah, nor in the case of America and *The Harbinger*. In neither case do the words and vows take place in a vacuum, but rather in the context of a nation in defiance of God. Nor is there any instance of man speaking into being what he wants to happen, much less creating a reality—but rather the very opposite. The words are a manifestation of that which already exists: a national spirit of defiance. Its utterance in America is significant as a manifestation and sealing, as a key event in the dynamic of progression involved in the replaying of the biblical template of judgment—but a dynamic and progression that originates not by the will of man. To compare a prosperity confession concerning a new Cadillac with a manifestation of biblical judgment is just about as ludicrous as it sounds.

A final charge against the Isaiah 9:10 Effect is the argument that unless one can name several different instances of a particular effect or dynamic taking place, then we can dismiss the effect. Really? We must ask the same question we've been asking all along of such critics—namely this: "From what rule book are you getting all these rules?" Certainly not from the Bible. And apparently not even from a dictionary. There is no such rule limiting the definition of an effect.

The critics go on to say that the Isaiah 9:10 Effect cannot be supported in the Bible. On the contrary, not only can it be supported, but also this very principle is actually cited in one form or another by Bible commentary after Bible commentary. In fact, one of the most classic, revered, and conservative of Bible commentaries cites the principle of Isaiah 9:10 as the template, the dynamic, the phenomenon, the effect, and the pattern of national and individual judgment.

The Mystery of the Shemitah

One critic attempts to negate the mystery of the Shemitah on the grounds that there are differences between the American financial implosion and what happened with ancient Israel, as if *The Harbinger* had ever presented the modern case as being exactly the same as the ancient case—which, of course, it never does. This reveals a confusion in the critic's understanding of what is actually being presented. *The Harbinger* never speaks of America being under the law of the Shemitah any more than it speaks of the harbingers as being the fulfillment of the ancient prophecy. On the contrary, *The Harbinger* clearly states that America is not under the law of the Shemitah or the fulfillment of Isaiah. Rather, it is the *signs* of national judgment and the *sign* of the Shemitah that is in effect.

777

One critic claims that *The Harbinger*'s citing of the 777 points wiped away in the crash of 2008 is false or misleading and that the actual number was 778 (talk about splitting hairs!). The claim is apparently based on his finding some citations or articles that reckoned the total at 778. The truth, however, is that the great crash of 2008 was, in fact, 777 points. There are always decimal points after such massive numbers, so there were a few who rounded the decimal points up to the next number, 778. But to use these few examples of rounding numbers to convince the hearer that *The Harbinger*'s citing of 777 points is misleading and deceptive is, itself, misleading and deceptive. Again, *The Harbinger*'s accuracy is upheld.

A Clash of Crashes

The critic then attempts to minimize the magnitude of what is universally recognized as the Great Recession. He cites that the assets and debts of the Lehman Brothers were just a small part of the world economy. The argument misses the point. The fall of Lehman Brothers, though massive in itself, was not the whole of the collapse but merely the trigger of the collapse that constituted the greatest economic disaster since the Great Depression.

The critic then attempts to downplay the scope of the collapse on September 29, 2008. He does this by stating that in terms of percentage, the crashes of the Great Depression were greater—and, by this argument, he labels the presentation of *The Harbinger* as an overstatement. The reader may thus be left with a false impression that the stock market collapse of 2008 was really not a major event.

Nothing could be further from the truth. The fact remains that it was the greatest stock-market-point crash in American history. That means even the crashes of the Great Depression were, in magnitude, smaller—much, much smaller—in comparison. In fact, even the great crash of Black Tuesday in 1929 added up to 38 points, which, in magnitude, amounts to a mere fraction of the 777 points that were wiped away in the crash of 2008.

The financial collapse of 2007–2008 involved over 7,000 points, wiping out years and years of economic activity and bringing the entire market to less than half its former volume. Had it been the other way around—had the mystery of *The Harbinger* involved the crash of the Great Depression instead of the crash of 2008—no doubt the critic would have protested that those earlier crashes were only "great" in terms of the relative value of percentage points and not the absolute value and magnitude, as in the much more colossal crash of 2008.

The Significant Fact

All such attacks and arguments serve only to hide the real issue: the Shemitah did indeed become a sign of judgment against a nation that had driven God out of its national life. The Shemitah did culminate on Elul 29, the day that the nation's financial accounts were wiped away. America is likewise a nation that has known God but is now expunging Him from its life. And the greatest financial crash in American history did indeed just happen to take place on the exact biblical day of the Shemitah—the twenty-ninth of Elul—when the financial accounts of a nation are wiped away.

Seven years before the greatest stock market crash in American history—September 2001—just happened to be the month of the other greatest crash in American history up to that date. And that other greatest crash in American and Wall Street history just happened to also take place on the same exact biblical day of the Shemitah—Elul 29—when the financial accounts of credit and debt are wiped away. Thus, the two greatest crashes in American history up to those dates each took place on the exact same biblical day, and on the one biblical day that just happens to be appointed to wipe away the financial accounts of a nation. On top of that, each took place seven years apart, which happens to be the period of the Shemitah, exactly seven years—seven biblical years to the exact biblical day!

As a Matter of Fact

These are anything but matters of statistics. These are facts that even most hardened or biased of skeptics must fight hard in an attempt to dismiss them. Just recently, before writing this answer to the critique, I just happened to come across a statistical analysis of this one fact in the mystery of the Shemitah. The analyst noted that he had taken a conservative and limited approach by not taking into account all the stock market trading days from the beginning—just those in the seven years between the crash of 2001 and the crash of 2008. His most conservative and limited conclusion? The chances of these two crashes happening when they did by chance comes out to, at the least, one chance in 1,361,899. Forget about overstatement—the reality is so stunning that it becomes impossible to overstate.

These are just some of the facts in *The Harbinger* that are never quite presented but obscured in one critic's critiques.

One blog posed an interesting question:

> The strangeness of the attacks against *The Harbinger* has to make you wonder what the devil has against it.[2]

A good question. What does the enemy have against *The Harbinger*? Most likely, a lot.

Chapter 6

The MEANING of the WORD

T<small>HE</small> H<small>ARBINGER</small> <small>DISCLOSES</small> the prophetic pattern being repeated in America regarding Isaiah 9:10. We can review this pattern from God's Word:

> The Lord sends a message against Jacob,
> And it falls on Israel.
> And all the people know it,
> That is, Ephraim and the inhabitants of Samaria,
> Asserting in pride and in arrogance of heart:
> "The bricks have fallen down,
> But we will rebuild with smooth stones;
> The sycamores have been cut down,
> But we will replace them with cedars."
> —I<small>SAIAH</small> 9:8–10

Prophecy or Pattern?

Some people have wondered if *The Harbinger* is taking the prophecy of Isaiah 9:10 out of its context.[1] The thought process that leads— incorrectly—to this line of questioning includes four assumptions that do not exist:

1. *The Harbinger* claims Isaiah 9:10 applies to America.

   Correction: *The Harbinger* does not make this claim; rather, it warns that Isaiah's prophecy, like many other prophecies throughout the Hebrew Bible (the Old Testament), forms a pattern of judgment established by God to deal with wayward nations, beginning with Israel and extending to all others. This is the biblical pattern for how God judges nations.

2. There can only be one way to understand Isaiah's prophecy, and it can be applied to only one historic event—ancient Israel's. Its application ends there.

   Correction: This assumption is incorrect because the biblical pattern is repeating itself in America today.

3. The literal and direct method of interpretation precludes any application of this prophecy or any other to any other historic event or situation.

   Correction: This assumption is also incorrect because the literal and direct method of interpretation is not the only method of interpretation in use.

4. No prophecy can be applied to more than one historic event and situation.

   Correction: This, as we shall demonstrate as we continue, is a flawed, man-made contrivance misused quite often theologically in order to support and advance a specific point of view.

The above four assumptions and the arguments used to support them are nothing but clever theological suppositions used to prevent people from identifying the prophetic pattern forming for America, which can be illustrated through the nine harbingers that have manifested themselves since 9/11, just as they did in ancient Israel.

"Whatever Was Written in Earlier Times Was Written for Our Instruction"

God has given us these wonderful stories so we might live better lives, not just so we might know more about what the Bible teaches. God didn't give us His truth to satisfy idle curiosity. He gave us His Word to change our lives.[2]

—CHARLES SWINDOLL

In his letter to Timothy, Paul wrote, "All Scripture is inspired[3] by God and profitable for teaching, for reproof, for correction, for training in righteousness; so that the man of God may be adequate, equipped for every good work" (2 Tim. 3:16–17).

Paul, in the Holy Spirit, wrote that the stories of the men and women of the Bible were written "for our sake also" (Rom. 4:24). In his instruction to the Roman church, he expanded on this thought by saying, "For whatever was written in earlier times was written for our instruction, so that through perseverance and the encouragement of the Scriptures we might have hope" (Rom. 15:4). As one example, remember the story of Abraham's life, which we read in our Bibles. God gave many promises to Abraham that carry an application for the children of God (Jewish and Gentile) who would come after Abraham and be encouraged and blessed by these promises. Consider the hope contained for all believers in just this one promise:

> ...Abraham will surely become a great and mighty nation, and in him all the nations of the earth will be blessed? For I have chosen him, so that he may command his children and his household after him to keep the way of the LORD by doing righteousness and justice, so that the LORD may bring upon Abraham what He has spoken about him.
>
> —GENESIS 18:18–19

Israel as Our Example

Elsewhere, the apostle Paul, in his first letter to the Corinthians, warns his readers to learn from Israel's example and not to make the same mistakes they did, telling them those things happened as examples for us so we would not crave the evil things they craved (1 Cor. 10:6). Later on Paul repeats himself, as if to punctuate the importance of this warning to learn from these examples (v. 11).

One of the psalmists captures the purpose of Scripture written so long ago as the timeless source of our inspiration:

> So the nations will fear the name of the LORD
> And all the kings of the earth Your glory.
> For the LORD has built up Zion;
> He has appeared in His glory.
> He has regarded the prayer of the destitute
> And has not despised their prayer.

This will be written for the generation to come,
That a people yet to be created may praise the
Lord.
—Psalm 102:15–18

Our Lord Jesus Himself has set the example
for us to follow (John 13:15). And where do we
get this example? In God's Word, the Bible. In
fact, the Holy Bible is the only book that is God-
breathed, and because of this, it is the only book
that reads us as we read it.

Through the Holy Spirit, the Word discloses
great and wonderful things about God and ourselves we would otherwise not know, as described
in the letter to the Hebrews:

> For the word of God is living and active and
> sharper than any two-edged sword, and piercing
> as far as the division of soul and spirit, of
> both joints and marrow, and able to judge the
> thoughts and intentions of the heart.
> —Hebrews 4:12

Additionally, it is understood by all Christians
that in order to understand the Bible and not read
something into it that's not there, one must first
be born again of the Spirit of God. Jesus reminded
the apostles of these things so they could write
them down (John 14:26), and it is He who teaches
us all things from what they wrote (1 John 2:27).

The Living Word

One of the key mistakes underlying the arguments of some critics is based on a fundamental
confusion. *The Harbinger* never says that Isaiah

is prophesying of America. Nor does it say that Isaiah is *also* speaking about America (in addition to ancient Israel). When it speaks of an ancient mystery, the mystery is that contained in Scripture concerning the manifestations and progression of national judgment. The dynamic is not that of an ancient prophecy being *fulfilled* in modern times, but of an ancient pattern of judgment being repeated in modern times. The repeating or replaying of biblical patterns is as grounded in Scripture as is the application of biblical examples and principles to daily life. Beyond that is another very basic dynamic, namely that God *uses* Scripture, and the principles of Scripture, to speak to His children and to man. And beyond that, Scripture itself is filled with examples of God taking one scripture that was clearly directed to one situation and meant for one context and applying it, using it, connecting to an entirely different situation and context.

The Passover Lamb and Dual Application

Let's have a look at one of these examples of fuller meaning, or *sensus plenior*.

Messiah was crucified between two criminals at Golgotha, where He died. The apostle John, writing under the inspiration of the Holy Spirit years later, indicated that Jesus' crucifixion took place on the specific day of preparation preceding the High Sabbath of the Feast of Unleavened Bread, which began at sundown on Wednesday that year (John 13:1).

Later, John mentions that the Pharisees

refused to go out to see Pilate in his judgment hall because they wanted to be able to partake in the Passover (John 18:28). This Sabbath was not a regular weekly Sabbath, but a High Sabbath, and for this reason, members of the Sanhedrin approached Pilate to request that his troops accelerate the deaths of those being crucified by breaking the prisoners' legs so they wouldn't remain on the crosses during the Sabbath and rot to death (John 19:31).

Pilate granted their requests, and the Romans broke the legs of the two prisoners on Jesus' either side. But when they came to Jesus, they didn't break His legs because they discovered He had already died.

To confirm His death, one of the soldiers pierced Jesus' side with a spear, and immediately blood and water came out. Then John says, "And he who has seen has testified, and his testimony is true; and he knows that he is telling the truth, so that you also may believe. For these things came to pass to fulfill the Scripture, 'NOT A BONE OF HIM SHALL BE BROKEN'" (vv. 35–36).

The apostle John, through the Holy Spirit, reveals a second application of an Old Testament scripture: The commandment in the Law concerning the Passover lamb (Exod. 12:1–28) was first fulfilled by the children of Israel eating the first Passover in Egypt the night before they were to leave for the Promised Land. In John 13 we see this scripture applied to the death of Messiah as the Passover Lamb.

So John applies specific examples from the

Hebrew Bible in the first Passover, in the Law, and in the Psalms as three prophetic witnesses of a historical event about which he writes as an eyewitness long after those events.

The Word and the Spirit

Elsewhere in John's Gospel our Lord gives us the key to the One who provides us with the ability to unlock the written and inspired Word of God and its meaning: "The [Holy] Spirit of truth…will guide you into all the truth" (John 16:13). Without the Holy Spirit, our understanding is darkened (1 Cor. 2:14–16), because unless we are born again, we cannot see or enter God's kingdom (John 3:3). The reality of the Holy Spirit's existence is nothing but a myth to the unregenerate mind.

The Pharisees, as well as the Sadducees, were conflicted about the Messiah and His origins, because when Nicodemus cited the Law as giving an accused person the right to testify on one's own behalf (John 7:50–51), implying the religious leaders were denying the Lord Jesus that right, they retorted by telling him to search the Scriptures because, according to them, "no prophet arises out of Galilee" (v. 52).

Now, take note. Jesus' detractors were not completely wrong in what they were saying, but they erred in their literal, minimalist method of interpretation. While it is true there was no direct prophecy stating the Messiah would come from Galilee, this did not prevent Him from visiting there in fulfillment of Isaiah's prophecy (Isa. 9:1).

The evangelists employ several verses from the prophets as direct fulfillments of Messianic prophecy related to these questions in their Gospels. (See, for example, Matthew 4:15.)

The Word of God is alive and active and sharper than any two-edged sword (Heb. 4:12), applicable and relevant to each generation regardless of the times, as long as it is understood correctly by those who read it in the Holy Spirit (John 14:16–17, 25–27).

Chapter 7

The ISAIAH 9:10
CONNECTION

THE *HARBINGER* FOLLOWS a biblical model by showing the application of Isaiah 9:10 in a modern context. Biblical events containing prophecies possess both historical and prophetic linear and parallel connections to one another. Allow me to define the meaning of *linear* and *parallel* in the context of prophetic scripture and its fulfillments throughout history.

+ A *linear* connection is one in which a specific prophecy is given and has a direct bearing upon and correlation with an event that takes place centuries later.

+ A *parallel* connection is one in which a specific prophecy has a dual fulfillment—one that takes place in the prophet's lifetime or generation and another that happens centuries later.

We see the evidence of this throughout the Bible, as events in both Testaments are tied to one another prophetically (linear) and in some cases understood in the paradigm of two completely unconnected historical events (parallel) connected prophetically at the place where the two events converge—or correlate—sometimes centuries apart from one another.

These are the best examples of where Scripture interprets Scripture, because we see the prophecy regarding a historical event given and then centuries later applied by the evangelists in their Gospels and in Acts and in the letters of the apostles, connecting the prophecies to specific events and situations within their lifetime.

We see prophecies partially fulfilled, right down to half of a verse, with the other half having its fulfillment at some future date. As to their interpretation, there are various schools of thought on that: amillennialist, premillennialist, postmillennialist, preterist, pretribulation, posttribulation, and so on.

One Internet site describes the duality of prophetic Scripture in the following manner:

> In fully understanding how the Bible utilizes this principle of "double fulfillment," one becomes armed against many Amillennial and Postmillennial objections. One will also begin to unlock many of the predictions the Bible has for the "last days."[1]

Regardless of what school of thought one hails from, none of these mitigate the fact that several prophecies are applicable and interpreted throughout the Scriptures in the context of more than one historical event, as we shall see.

Additionally, the reader will note that in many

instances, the historical events have absolutely no connection with each other, nor can one ascertain the literal meaning of the prophecy to connect it to the second historical event unless reading about it through the pages of the evangelists who interpret them as such.

The Jonah Template and the Resurrection

Take, for example, the story of Jonah. He flees God's calling on his life and is swallowed by a large marine animal and spends three nights within its bowels. The fish vomits Jonah onto the shore.

In the New Testament, the Lord Jesus applies this story to His own death, burial for three days, and resurrection (Matt 12:38–40). This again is a specific example of biblical *exegesis* where a scripture and scriptural patterns are applied to an event different from that of its original context.

The Sign of Immanuel

Let's look at a few examples from the Hebrew Bible and their fulfillment in the pages of the New Testament.

Isaiah 7:14, as applied to Matthew 1:18–25

After Solomon's reign, during the years of the divided kingdoms of Israel[2] and Judah,[3] in the days of Jotham, the Syrian-Samaritan alliance had come against Judah with the intention of replacing Judah's King Ahaz with Syria-Samaria's own puppet king, who would be more amenable to their wishes (2 Kings 15:37; Isa. 7:5–9).

It was during this time that the word of the

Lord came to the prophet Isaiah, and he challenged King Ahaz to ask God for a sign, saying the king could "make it deep as Sheol or high as heaven" (Isa. 7:11). But when Ahaz refused to test God by asking Him for a sign to help strengthen his faith, at God's explicit command through Isaiah the prophet, he was given a sign that indicated his enemy would soon be removed (v. 16).

What was the sign? That an adolescent Jewish woman of marriageable age would bear a son and name him Immanuel—which means "God with us" (v. 14).

Now move several centuries into the future to sometime around 6 BC, when Jesus' mother, Mary, was betrothed to Joseph. Before they had consummated their marriage, she was found to be with child by the Holy Spirit, which Matthew attributes to be a direct fulfillment of Isaiah's prophecy to Ahaz (Matt. 1:18–25).

Two distinct, completely unconnected historical events are connected by a single prophetic verse of Scripture whose literal sense and meaning indicate two completely different things, except when intersected with the latter historical event—Jesus' miraculous conception by the Holy Spirit and His birth.

My Son Out of Egypt

Hosea lived in the northern kingdom in the eighth century BC during the reign of Jeroboam. His contemporary was Amos the prophet, who also prophesied to the northern kingdom, though he was from Tekoa, a town about six miles north-east of Bethlehem of Judah.

In the Book of Hosea, God describes how He loved the people of Israel as His own son since Israel's youth and mentions the nation's exodus out of Egypt as an example of how He loved and cared for Israel (Hosea 11:1), even though Israel sacrificed to Baal and bowed to graven images (v. 2). Israel was enslaved in Egypt, and the Lord God brought him whom He calls "My son" out, because He loved His people as though they were His own son.

Now move several centuries into the future, to about 4 BC, the time of Herod the Great's death. In his Gospel, Matthew writes that upon hearing news of Herod's death (Matt. 2:19–23), Mary and Joseph returned from Egypt with Jesus. Matthew quotes from Hosea's prophecy concerning God's calling His Son out of Egypt (v. 15).

Here again, we see two distinct, completely unconnected historical events connected by a single prophetic verse of Scripture, whose literal sense and meaning indicate two completely different things except when intersected with the latter historical event—Jesus' return to the land of Israel.

The Tears of Rachel

Our third example is even greater in contrast, as we shall see. The Babylonian exile was so seared into the hearts and minds of the Jewish people that ninety years after the tragic event, Jeremiah, who lived around the year 627 BC, raised a loud, prophetic lamentation over his people and their plight in Ramah.[4]

Ramah was a settlement in the area of Gibeon and Beeroth (Josh. 18:25), approximately five miles north of Jerusalem. Jeremiah was released from prison in Ramah (Jer. 39:11–14; 40:1). Earlier in his ministry he had described seeing Rachel, who was buried in Ramah (Gen. 35:19; 49:7; 1 Sam. 10:2), weeping bitterly for her children (Jer. 31:15). The allusion goes back to the times of the patriarchs. Rachel had been barren until she gave birth to Joseph and Benjamin. She died just as her son Benjamin was born (Gen. 35:18). The descendants of Benjamin, the Benjamites,[5] were taken into exile into Babylon in 722 BC. (The land of Gibeon, Ramah, Bethlehem, and Beeroth was within the territory that had been given to Benjamin, Rachel's son.[6])

Now move several centuries into the future as King Herod the Great approaches the close of his reign. Matthew's Gospel records that Herod ordered the slaughter of Bethlehem's children who were two years old and younger (Matt. 2:16–18). This type of brutality from Herod is attested to by Josephus and other historians of the period.

We see here two distinct, completely unconnected historical events connected by a single prophetic verse of Scripture whose literal sense and meaning indicate two completely different things, except when intersected with the latter historical event, which was Herod's genocidal act of slaughtering Bethlehem's innocents.

In this example we see not one but two

examples of a scripture being reused and applied
by the Spirit of God—Rachel's death near Bethlehem, the calamity of the Babylonian captivity, and
the slaughter in the same place by King Herod at
the time of Messiah's infancy. Clearly, the reuse
and reapplication of Scripture and scriptural patterns is not only something God *can* do, but also
something He often does.

Hagar Is Mt. Sinai

To sum up, a fundamental error of interpretation
has been made by some critics upon which everything falls—namely that *The Harbinger* is saying
that events in America are *the fulfillment* or *a fulfillment* of Isaiah. This one foundational error and
confusion results in further errors and confusions
built upon yet further errors and confusions.

In order to attack *The Harbinger*, one would
have to argue either that God has not, cannot, or
does not use scriptures in one context to apply
to another. As to "has not," the critic would be
authoritatively speaking for God, which is the very
thing that these particular critics accuse others of
doing. As to "cannot," clearly that would contradict basic theology. We are left with "does not."
The problem with "does not" is that the entire
Bible contradicts such an accusation. Again, again,
and again, God uses one scripture, one scriptural
event, one scriptural pattern to speak of other
events and occurrences.

Further, He affirms and anoints this very thing
in the writings of His people. If a critic argues
that the Old Testament scriptures quoted by

the gospel writer are different in that one could argue that they were meant from the beginning to speak of Messiah, the critic has missed the point. The point is that God clearly makes use of Scripture and scriptural examples. The natural context and interpretation thereof are clearly very different than what it is now being applied to. If the critic argues that God knew from the beginning that He would use the verse in Hosea, clearly speaking of Israel's exodus from Egypt to one day apply to Messiah, we would agree. The problem is God knows how every scripture will be used and applied from here to eternity. He even knows how He can and will use and apply every scripture. All the more, the argument that God cannot use the national warning of Isaiah 9 to another nation in danger of judgment holds no biblical water.

The Bible is overflowing with examples. One cannot read the writing of Paul without recognizing this principle.

What Paul writes that "the Hagar is Mt. Sinai in Arabia...," he's stating that Abraham's maid, Hagar, is a mountain. Is this the original meaning of the account of Hagar...or, for that matter, the account of Mt. Sinai? No. But the Spirit of God is joining them together and using them to reveal a spiritual or prophetic message.

In 1 Corinthians 9 Paul speaks of the right of ministers to be blessed with the fruit of their ministry. In verse 9 he writes, "It is written in the Law of Moses, 'You shall not muzzle the mouth of an ox that treads the grain." He goes on to say that this verse was written for us, *concerning God's ministers.* One can only imagine what such critics would say had they been around in the first century confronted with the writings of Paul. Using such workings, they would have torn him apart while accusing him of twisting the scriptures, taking them completely out of context, using them for his own ends, committing hermeneutical heresy, etc., etc.

The fact is God uses scriptures all the time to speak to His children and to speak to them in situations far removed from that of the original context of those scriptures. If it were not so, virtually every pastor would have to resign and virtually every church close its doors. Not only does God use and reuse scriptures to apply to varied situations, but He does so in specific detail—in the lives of His children and in Scripture itself.

The Surprise: God Uses His Word!

The Harbinger affirms that what is being seen in America is a repetition of what occurred in ancient Israel. What we are witnessing is a pattern of prophetic warning and judgment. It is a pattern in Bible prophecy that is based on Isaiah 9:10 and specific to the nation of Israel, yet it holds significance for America because of the pattern of judgment that came to ancient Israel.

Because America was founded on Judeo-Christian principles, inasmuch as it was consecrated to God in prayer upon its founding, it has been blessed by the Lord abundantly more than any nation except Israel. America also has been used by God to spread the Word around the world. These reasons help in identifying how this pattern of prophetic warning and judgment is being replayed in America today.

The pattern of warning and the nation's reaction to that warning is being repeated, and the evidence shows it. It is the choice of those who read about it to either believe it or disregard it, as these people do. The choice is left to them.

The Harbinger fully affirms that the context of Isaiah 9:10 applies to ancient Israel. Thus, it does not change in any way the traditional hermeneutics or interpretation of the Scriptures. In fact, it expounds on the ancient context again and again. But *The Harbinger* reveals that the pattern, the template, and the progression of judgment manifested in the last days of ancient Israel are now manifesting again in twenty-first-century America.

The dynamic of *The Harbinger* derives from a very basic and sound foundation. God judges the sins of nations. God warns of His judgment. And God is consistent in His actions. Thus He warns and judges in a way consistent with His nature, His acts, and His Word. So should it surprise us that God should use a biblical pattern of warning and judgment to speak to a nation in danger of judgment? Of course not. Should He warn from another book...from the Quran...from *The Communist Manifesto*? In other words, if God uses prophecies, patterns, examples, symbols, and images continuously to apply to more than one event, person, or context, then for Him to use a biblical template of national judgment to warn a modern nation of national judgment makes extreme sense. It would be far more surprising if God, in warning a nation that was founded on His Word, would, in that warning, fail to use His Word.

The Greatest Blasphemy

We've pondered what would happen if these same critics were alive in the time of Paul and applied the same strategies. What if they had been around at the time when the Gospel accounts had just come out? What if they had only known the Old Testament and had applied the same critical tactics? We can only imagine how zealously they would have condemned the Gospel writers—Matthew for ripping a passage about the Exodus out of context and twisting it to apply to the Messiah, John for taking a passage concerning the bones of the Passover lamb and claiming it applied to the Messiah's death, Luke for applying the prophesies of Isaiah to the ministering of the apostles, etc. etc.

And what would they have done to Messiah—a man who quoted ancient scriptures to apply to Himself? Well, we know what others did to Him. They were those who set themselves up as keepers of the truth and who used the letter of the law to condemn while missing the spirit of the law and the moving of God's hand. The problem with these approaches to God's Word and works is that they tend, again and again, to miss the very God they claim to uphold. In the name of upholding God's ways, they tend to be prone to committing the greatest blasphemy of all. They miss God's work. They miss God's heart. They miss His presence. They miss His voice. They miss His call. And worst of all, when He comes in their midst...they tend to crucify Him.

Chapter 8

PROPHECY, PATTERN,
or COINCIDENCE?

I'VE DISCUSSED THE pattern being repeated in previous chapters. Allow me to recap briefly here and then go a bit deeper in our understanding of what has been taking place.

Senator Tom Daschle, in his capacity as Senate majority leader, spoke before the US Senate on September 12, 2001, in our nation's capital, he chose one single verse to quote from the Bible, and that verse was Isaiah 9:10. He applied that verse to the tragic events that had befallen the nation the previous day.

Some years later, on September 11, 2004, Senator John Edwards, while running as vice president on John Kerry's bid for the White House, spoke before a gathering of the Congressional Black Caucus held to commemorate the tragic events of September 11. The scripture he chose to read was Isaiah 9:10.

When President Obama spoke before a joint session of Congress commemorating the tragic events of September 11 in his State of the Union address in 2009, he unwittingly repeated and paraphrased the words of this same scripture—Isaiah 9:10.

All of these events took place independently of one another. They all took place in our nation's capital. They all commemorated September 11. They all used the prophecy of Isaiah 9:10 and connected it to September 11.

All three men in all three incidents did this long before *The Harbinger* was written.

+ Fact: The nation's highest leaders spoke.

+ Fact: It happened.

+ Fact: It happened in our nation's capital.

+ Fact: It happened, on all three occasions, within the halls of Congress—within the Capitol building itself.

There is absolutely no way anyone could have contrived to carry these events out, nor were they the invention of anyone's imagination. *The Harbinger* simply records the events. The connections to 9/11 are made by the events that followed 9/11 and by those taking part in them. *The Harbinger* only bears this out. It did not invent them, and it did not bring them to pass; the events happened independently of one another and independently of any human effort to intentionally bring them to pass.

Even the people involved in them were not made to take part in them by anyone's will but only their own will within God's will, divine providence, and sovereignty.

All three men quoted the prophecy from Isaiah and, using the words of the prophecy, vowed to apply it to the nation's rebuilding, replanting, and restoration at Ground Zero—affirming their commitment that it would get done.

The Caiaphas Pattern

The connection is a prophetic pattern of events following one after the other and tied by the prophecy itself. In this case, its quoting and application (knowingly or unknowingly) by the nation's leaders occur in the same manner as the biblical example of Caiaphas, who spoke prophetically, according to John's Gospel, in his capacity as high priest by saying that Jesus had to die rather than the nation perish (John 11:47–53).

As I mentioned in chapter 4, the high priest Caiaphas did not realize he spoke in a prophetic capacity, yet regardless of his being aware of it or not, his words were taken by the evangelists as prophetic when they wrote their Gospels under the inspiration of the Holy Spirit.

This is scriptural evidence of a prophetic utterance unknowingly being made by one who is not himself a prophet, but because of authority of the office he holds as leader of his nation, he speaks prophetically of something that comes to pass.

This same pattern holds true of the three occasions in which Isaiah 9:10 has been applied by our nation's leaders in our nation's capital, all tied directly to the events of September 11, 2001, vowing to do the same as the vow in that prophecy. All three men on each of the three occasions within the halls of the US Capitol made the declaration and applied the vow from the prophecy while making it official US policy to do the same. In this act, they pronounced the judgment that triggered the harbingers.

Additionally, there have been other public officials who have continued to vow the nation's determination to rebuild, replant, and recover from the effects of 9/11 without once giving deference to God or questioning whether there should be a national day of prayer for repentance.

The Reality Problem: It Happened!

Jonathan Cahn did not connect the event of 9/11 or the words of the three leaders to the prophetic verse of Scripture in Isaiah 9:10—these three leaders did. And—I repeat—they did so before he wrote his book.

These leaders' vow of defiance against the devastation, against those who committed these atrocities, and against the event itself and their commitment to rebuild, replant, and restore the grounds where the calamity took place has become as the vow made twenty-seven hundred years earlier in Israel—a declaration of judgment against the nation making it. Not only did they repeat the ancient vow, but they also did so without committing the nation's rebuilding efforts to God, thus completely excluding Him as though He had no role to play in its recovery.

Those who criticize *The Harbinger* have overlooked the fact that these events did, in fact, occur and are now a matter of history. Jonathan Cahn did not create these events as the plot and storyline of his narrative. All of them occurred—just as he describes them—before he wrote his book. This is a glaring oversight in the dialogue of the people who criticize *The Harbinger* and its author.

The events of September 11, 2001, have been thoroughly documented. Many documentaries have been produced, telling and retelling the same story with various details from many different angles. Many testimonials and personal recollections by those who lived it and survived it have become a matter of public record.

Both what happened on that terrible day and what preceded it has been investigated thoroughly. Even what has happened since that day has been reported by the various news organizations and print media with regard to the rebuilding of the Freedom Tower.

Moreover, in the context of Isaiah's prophecy, the bricks are a metaphor for reconstruction, of the rebuilding of edifices that have fallen. So too are the hewn stones to replace the fallen bricks and the replanting of cedars in place of the sycamore. The determination to build better, bigger, and taller affirms the nation's leaders' obstinate determination to accomplish this at any cost without any accountability to God for their efforts.

The bricks, wood, and steel of the World Trade Center have fallen, but the rebuilding began in earnest with hewn stone on July 4, 2004, when the granite cornerstone for the building of the Freedom Tower was set. There was a great ceremony surrounding the event, and again the vows were repeated.[1]

As I mentioned before, the sycamore tree

outside Saint Paul's Chapel fell when it was struck and uprooted by the beam and debris from the collapsing World Trade Center towers, but a cedar (*erez*) tree was lowered into place on November 22, 2003. It was named the Tree of Hope. This so-called Tree of Hope today is shriveled and is close to death.

No one was orchestrating these things—they just happened.

A Mind-Boggling Mystery: The Shemitah

You may be wondering, "What exactly is the Shemitah?" Allow me to explain.

When the children of Israel settled the Holy Land, they began to count and observe seven-year cycles; the end of each seven-year period would culminate with a sabbatical year known as the Shemitah. The Shemitah year waived all outstanding debts between Jewish debtors and creditors. Everything was wiped clean (Deut. 15:1–2). During that year, all agricultural activity would cease, and for a year the land was allowed to replenish and restore itself (Lev. 25:3–6).

Of what significance is that to the United States? I quote from *The Harbinger Companion With Study Guide*:

> The greatest collapse of the 2008 economic implosion and the greatest stock market crash in American history happened on September 29, 2008. That day on the biblical calendar was the twenty-ninth day of Elul, the final, crowning day of the Hebrew Shemitah—and the exact

day appointed by God for the wiping away of a nation's financial accounts.

The Shemitah revolves around the number seven. So the number seven arises over and over again concerning the economic collapse of 2008. The great collapse happened on the crowning day of the seventh year. It was triggered on Capitol Hill when Congress rejected a $700 billion bailout plan. Seven percent of the market was wiped out. And the number of points wiped away was 777.[2]

In 2008, $1.2 trillion were lost and the stock market dropped almost 778 points.[3] By October, the next month, the Dow Jones Industrial's prolonged fifteen-month tumble wiped out Americans of $2 trillion dollars in retirement savings.[4] In five years, more than half of the value of our money evaporated by inflation.

Coincidence or providence? Happenstance or God's sovereignty? You be the judge. But the Scriptures teach there is no such thing as coincidence, chance, or luck; rather, they teach that God is intricately involved in our lives (Ps. 138:7–8; Matt. 10:28–30; Luke 12:6–7; Rom. 8:28; Eph. 1:11; 2 Tim. 4:18) and with nations and kingdoms (Rom. 9:28).

In fact, there is no such thing as coincidence in Judaism, and there is no Hebrew word for *coincidence*, because it means that something happened by itself. Anyone with a rudimentary knowledge of Scripture understands that the Holy Bible does not teach coincidences.

This sovereignty of God is called *Hashgacha*

Pratis. One Jewish writer says that it "runs every single miniscule aspect of our (and everyones') lives. Therefore, there is nothing that happens without His direct involvement and doing."[5]

Signs Given to Confirm God's Hand

The children of Israel were slaves in Egypt, but when God delivered them from Pharaoh's hand, He did so with great signs and wonders, plagues, and pestilence. He divided up the Red Sea before them, and they walked on dry ground. He fed them in the wilderness and provided for all their needs for a period of forty years, until that generation had died and no one but Joshua and Caleb were left. Were these coincidences or the hand of almighty God?

When God gave Joshua a long day so that the children of Israel would defeat the combined armies of five Amorite kings in 1400 BC, so that the sun stood still and the moon stopped until the nation avenged itself of its enemies (Josh 10:11–13), was it a coincidence or was it a sign of God's providence and sovereignty?

And shall we call what happened in the reign of Hezekiah, when the shadow on Ahaz's sundial retreated ten degrees (2 Kings 20:11),[6] a coincidence or a sign of the providence and sovereignty of God?

Was what happened to Nebuchadnezzar, king of Babylon, a mere coincidence, when God took away his reasoning for a period of time until he acknowledged the sovereignty of God and recognized that the Most High is ruler over the realm of mankind and bestows it on whomever He wishes (Dan. 4:25)? Was it a coincidence when he did not have his reasoning restored to him until he raised his eyes toward heaven and his reason returned to him and he blessed the Most High and praised and honored Him who lives forever? When he acknowledged God's sovereignty over nations, kingdoms, and people, and God restored his kingdom and made him great?

Was it a coincidence or the hand of God that after two thousand years of exile and persecution, the Jewish people returned to their ancestral homeland, founded the modern state of Israel in one day, on May 14, 1948, in fulfillment of prophecy (Isa. 66:8–9), resurrected Hebrew as a modern language,[7] and on June 7, 1967, recaptured Jerusalem—all within less than a generation?

Is it a coincidence that the following has occurred to Israel on the ninth day of the lunar Hebrew month of Av throughout history?

- On the ninth of Av in the year 1313 BC, the children of Israel cried to God their wish to return to Egypt. For this, that generation did not enter the Promised Land. Of that group, only Joshua and Caleb entered the land.

- On the ninth of Av, the first temple was destroyed. Five hundred years later, the second temple was destroyed on the ninth of Av in the year AD 70.

♦ On the ninth of Av in AD 133, the Romans defeated the armies of the false messiah Ben Kosibah at the final Battle of Betar.

♦ On August 15, 1096—the ninth of Av—the First Crusade officially began. In the first month of this crusade, 10,000 were killed in France and the Rhineland. More than 1.2 million Jews were murdered by marauding crusaders in this crusade.

♦ The Jews were expelled from England on the ninth of Av in the year 1290.

♦ The Jews were expelled from France on the ninth of Av of 1306.

♦ Spain's Golden Age ended on the ninth of Av in the year 1492, when Queen Isabella and King Ferdinand expelled Spain's Jews.

♦ World War II and the Holocaust, historians conclude, was actually the long, drawn-out conclusion of World War I, which began in 1914 on the ninth of Av. This tragic day is known in Judaism as Tisha B'Av.

♦ On August 2, 1941—the ninth of Av—SS Commander Heinrich Himmler was given the approval to commence the *final solution*, in which half of the world's Jews were murdered by the Nazis. On July

23, 1942—also the ninth of Av—the
mass deportation of Jews began from the
Warsaw ghetto to Treblinka.

Is it a coincidence that despite repeated attempts
by empires, kingdoms, nations, and people more
powerful and more numerous than they, the only
ancient people to live into the modern era are the
Jewish people? Is it coincidence or the faithfulness
and sovereignty of God?

The Non-Coincidental Hand of God

When faced with the question of whether these
amazing occurrences are purely happenstance—
things that happened at random all by
themselves—we come to the realization of God's
sovereignty and providence, as well as His grace.
Nothing happens by chance, but rather by the
providence and sovereignty of almighty God and
His foreknowledge and redemptive plan for mankind, beginning with Israel and extending out
through the cross to the entire human race.

The harbingers have appeared to warn us of
judgment as our nation passes the tipping point, of
which our leaders and popular culture seem obliv-
ious. The nation sleeps as it careens toward God's
imminent judgment. Where are God's people in
all this? Are we sounding the alarm? Blowing the
trumpet? Calling our nation to repentance? Or
are we too busy criticizing each other over triviali-
ties? You be the judge.

SECTION II

DEEPER EXPLANATIONS
OF THE TRUTH OF
THE HARBINGER

Chapter 9

The TRUTH ABOUT AMERICA'S FOUNDING

A MERICA, THE LAND upon which the United States was founded, was a land repeatedly dedicated to God by the Puritans, who prayed to the Almighty that He bless their communities and the land around them. The Pilgrims, in their Mayflower Compact, established through prayer their covenant with almighty God for the establishment of their communities for the propagation of the gospel of Jesus and more—much more.

In this chapter we take a brief backward look to rediscover the unique role that the gospel and its propagation had upon America—a role that is evident both before and after the land was settled, and later, when its colonies won their independence from England and became the United States of America.

From the very beginning, many of those who settled the land were committed to bring the gospel of Jesus to it and to share the gospel with its native population. This is not to say there were no unscrupulous or evil men among those who settled the land, because there were. But unlike other European settlers, who sought to conquer the New World by means of their military charge and to pillage it for gold, among the first English settlers were also committed Christians who sought to bring Jesus and His gospel to the natives of this vast wilderness called America.

Here is where the story of America's founding begins.

The Founding of America's Colonies

America was not founded on July 4, 1776, but on April 29, 1607, at a place that was called by its settlers Cape Henry, which is now the seacoast Virginia Beach on the Atlantic Ocean. When King James commissioned the Virginia Charter, he had quite an expansive view of what that land was going to comprise.

British geographer and writer Richard Hakluyt was fired up with the desire to bring the gospel of Jesus to the shores of the New World and to settle it. He was responsible for writing and publishing the records of the chief travelers and settlers in North America during the fifteenth and sixteenth centuries.

Hakluyt gathered together a group of a total of eight men, called the Virginia Company, and they asked the king for territory.[1] The First Virginia Charter issued by James I in 1606 gave the London Company the right to "*begin theire plantacions and habitacions in some fitt and conveniente place between fower and thirtie and one and fortie degrees of the said latitude all alongest the coaste of Virginia and coastes of America.*"[2] The area between 34 and 41 degrees latitude stretches from present-day South Carolina to New York City.

It was an enormous tract of land the king gave them, and it is what we know now as Virginia, a name that originated with Queen Elizabeth I, who was known as the Virgin Queen. This land—Virginia—was named after her. It is said that Sir Walter Raleigh was responsible for naming the land.

Richard Hakluyt was an ordained minister. This man felt the calling of God to bring the gospel to peoples of the continent of North America.[3] He was responsible for asking Robert Hunt, a young parish priest in the Church of England, to be the chaplain of the new colony. Leaving his wife, Elizabeth Edwards, and children, Thomas and Elizabeth, behind, Hunt went about the journey—a treacherous one. He would never see his wife and children again,[4] but he was the glue that God used to hold the band of disparate crewmen together on the journey. Three ships were commissioned for the journey to settle the new land.

The Planting of America

On April 25, after a long and treacherous journey of 144 days without sight of land, the captain and his crew discussed whether or not they should return to England. But the next day they sighted land in what would come to be called the Chesapeake Bay. Quickly they got off board their ships and made their way to shore, making landfall on the twenty-sixth of April 1607.

The land was full of wild berries, and they were able to harvest oysters, but there were still divisions among the crew. Hunt told them he would not allow them to get off their boats until they reconciled with one another and with the Lord. For the next three days they did just that. The date was April 29, 1607.

After this, Hunt wrote, "Now we can go forth," and they took a seven-foot oak cross and planted it firmly on the land they were about to settle. The land on which they planted this cross is today known as Virginia Beach. They named it *Cape Henry*, after the eldest son of King James I of England, the king who commissioned what is the most-beloved Bible, known in the English language as the King James Bible.

And what shall we say of the Puritans who came and settled the land, and of the Pilgrims who came later, and of the stories behind these, all of which tell of a people in flux and a faith in action, as more and more Christians settled the land, some to separate from the Church of England while others came to bring the church to these shores? They all believed their primary mission was to bring the gospel to these lands and to establish strong Christian communities across the North American continent.

Because our primary concern is with the founding of the United States, we must continue to move on to the eighteenth century and the American Revolution and the founding of the American republic we know as the United States of America, a nation unlike any before it or since in history.

The Story of America and the
American Revolution

When the War for Independence began, George Washington was selected as general of the army of the United States. The day after he took charge, he issued orders, requiring "all officers and soldiers not engaged in actual duty to attend Divine Services to implore blessings of heaven upon the means used for their safety and defense."[5]

There are many stories regarding the various miraculous deliverances accorded the American forces under Washington's command and his continual reliance on the Almighty. These stories show evidence that Washington constantly relied on prayer to the Lord God. On one occasion, we can see the amazing answer that followed.

The British had the Colonials almost completely surrounded in a giant semicircle with their backs to the East River, and the situation appeared hopeless and dire because all land routes were blocked by the British. The only exit route was through the mile-wide East River. But providential "adverse weather conditions kept British ships from sailing up the East River,"[6] therefore preventing the British from establishing a naval blockade.

This allowed Washington to attempt to evacuate his forces from the island in secrecy. He ordered the collection of every rowboat, sailboat, and worthy seagoing vessel to be collected, and on the night of August 29, 1776, at 8:00 p.m., he ordered the evacuation of his forces from Long Island.

Both heavy rains and adverse winds hindered the British ships from intercepting Washington's forces as they retreated. By 11:00 p.m., the northeast wind that had raged for three days ceased, and "the water became so calm that the boats could be loaded with extra weight. A gentle breeze arose from the South and Southwest, which favored their travel across the river to New York."[7]

The retreat continued throughout the night and well into the pre-dawn hours of the following day, yet there were still countless of numbers of troops that needed to be evacuated. Their death appeared imminent, but the records of Major Benjamin Talmage say that something astonishing happened. The following are his own words describing it:

> After dawn of the next day approached, those of us who remained in the trenches became very anxious for our own safety and when the dawn appeared there were several regiments here on duty. At this time, a very dense fog began to rise out of the ground and off the river. It seemed to settle in a peculiar manner over both encampments. I recollect this peculiar Providential occurrence perfectly well. And so very dense was the atmosphere that I could scarcely discern a man six yards distance. We tarried until the sun had risen but the fog remained as dense as ever.[8]

The fog did not lift until the last boats left Long Island. Then something else happened that proved providential. When the fog began to lift, British troops were hurriedly dispatched to the river, but when they arrived on the scene, all they saw were four boats on the river, with the nearest one containing three vagabonds who had remained behind to plunder whatever they could scavenge for themselves. Thousands of men and materials had successfully evacuated by then. American General Greene said that this was "the best effective retreat [he] ever read or heard of!" This event was so astonishing that surely the explanation given by many of the colonists was true: "God was defending the cause of liberty."[9]

During the course of the War for Independence, the American Colonialists fighting for independence continued to pray for God's providential favor, and it was often that General Washington would be found on his knees in the woods, praying for the cause of liberty. There is a prayer room in the Capitol building where, on a stained-glass window, the figure of George Washington can be seen kneeling in prayer, and behind him is a prayer from the sixteenth psalm, saying, "Preserve me, Oh Lord, for in Thee do I put my trust."

We have the following from the Historic Valley Forge website, in an article titled "Washington's 'Earnest Prayer'":

Washington's "Earnest Prayer"

The following prayer was written by General Washington at the close of the War for Independence on June 14, 1783, in Newburgh, New York, and distributed to the thirteen governors of the newly free states in the form of a "Circular

Letter Addressed to the Governors of all the States on the Disbanding of the Army."

Circular Letter Addressed to the Governors of all the States on the Disbanding of the Army, June 14, 1783

I have thus freely declared what I wished to make known, before I surrendered up my public trust to those who committed it to me. The task is now accomplished. I now bid adieu to your Excellency, as the chief magistrate of your State, at the same time I bid a last farewell to the cares of office and all the employments of public life.

It remains, then, to be my final and only request that your Excellency will communicate these sentiments to your legislature at their next meeting, and that they may be considered the legacy of one, who has ardently wished, on all occasions, to be useful to his country, and who, even in the shade of retirement, will not fail to implore the divine benediction on it.

I now make it my earnest prayer that God would have you, and the State over which you preside, in his holy protection; that he would incline the hearts of the citizens to cultivate a spirit of subordination and obedience to government, to entertain a brotherly affection and love for one another, for their fellow-citizens of the United States at large, and particularly for brethren who have served in the field; and finally that he would most graciously be pleased to dispose us all to do justice, to love mercy, and to demean ourselves with that charity, humility, and pacific temper of mind, which were the characteristics of the Divine Author of our blessed religion, and without an humble imitation of whose example in these things, we can never hope to be a happy nation.[10]

There is more about the father of our country, George Washington, found in his morning prayer journal. I quote:

Monday Morning Prayer

O eternal and everlasting God, I presume to present myself this morning before thy Divine majesty, beseeching thee to accept of my humble and hearty thanks, that it hath pleased thy great goodness to keep and preserve me the night past from all the dangers poor mortals are subject to, and has given me sweet and pleasant sleep, whereby I find my body refreshed and comforted for performing the duties of this day, in which I beseech thee to defend me from all perils of body and soul.

Direct my thoughts, words and work. Wash away my sins in the immaculate blood of the lamb, and purge my heart by thy Holy Spirit, from the dross of my natural corruption, that I may with more freedom of mind and liberty of will serve thee, the everlasting God, in righteousness and holiness this day, and all the days of my life.

Increase my faith in the sweet promises of the Gospel. Give me repentance from dead works. Pardon my wanderings, & direct my thoughts unto thyself, the God of my salvation. Teach me how to live in thy fear, labor in thy service, and ever to run in the ways of thy commandments. Make me always watchful over my heart, that neither the terrors of conscience, the loathing of

holy duties, the love of sin, nor an unwillingness
to depart this life, may cast me into a spiritual
slumber. But daily frame me more and more into
the likeness of thy son Jesus Christ, that living
in thy fear, and dying in thy favor, I may in thy
appointed time attain the resurrection of the
just unto eternal life. Bless my family, friends &
kindred unite us all in praising & glorifying thee
in all our works begun, continued, and ended,
when we shall come to make our last account
before thee blessed Saviour, who hath taught us
thus to pray, our Father.[11]

No man who prays in such a manner from
his heart can be turned away—and what's more,
Jesus Himself has promised universally to all men
everywhere that He would never turn them away
(John 6:37).

The Inauguration

At his first inauguration, George Washington
took the oath of office on April 30, 1789. When
he took the oath of office, he was standing on the
balcony of Federal Hall in New York City. He
placed his hand on an open Bible borrowed from
the local Masonic Lodge, because they had forgotten to bring one to the inauguration.[12]

A critic of *The Harbinger* pointed out that this
Bible was a Masonic Bible, but this only indicates that it is one that was available quickly at
the inaugural event when it was discovered that
none had been secured before the event. This borrowed Bible was housed at the St. John Masonic
Lodge only a few hundred feet down the block.[13]

The most commonly used version in use among Masonic Lodges is the King James Bible.

When George Washington finished taking the oath, he made the following declaration, which I quote in part here:

> Such being the impressions under which I have, in obedience to the public summons, repaired to the present station; it would be peculiarly improper to omit, in this first official Act, my fervent supplications to that Almighty Being who rules over the Universe, who presides in the Councils of Nations, and whose providential aide can supply every human defect, that His benediction may consecrate to the liberties and happiness of the People of the United States, a Government....In tendering this homage to the Great Author of every public and private good I assure myself that it expresses your sentiments not less than my own; nor those of my fellow-citizens at large, less than either. No People can be bound to acknowledge and adore the invisible hand, which conducts the Affairs of men more than the People of the United States. Every step, by which they have advanced to the character of an independent nation, seems to have been distinguished by some token of providential agency...from which the event has resulted, cannot be compared with the means by which most Governments have been established, without some return of pious gratitude along with an humble anticipation of the future blessings which the past seem to presage....
>
> We ought to be no less persuaded that the propitious smiles of Heaven, can never be expected on a nation that disregards the eternal

rules of order and right, which Heaven itself has ordained: And since the preservation of sacred fire of liberty, and the destiny of the Republican model of Government, are justly considered as deeply, perhaps as finally staked, on the experiment…

I shall take my present leave; but not without resorting once more to the benign parent of the human race, in humble supplication that since he has been pleased to favour the American people, with opportunities for deliberating in perfect tranquility, and dispositions for deciding with unparalleled unanimity on a form of Government, for the security of their Union, and the advancement of their happiness; so his divine blessings may be equally *conspicuous* in the enlarged views, the temperate consultations, and the wise measures on which the success of this Government must depend.[14]

Afterward, the new president and all who were members of the new government—a joint session of Congress—walked from Federal Hall to a little church named Saint Paul's Chapel located on the grounds where Ground Zero is now located, and there they prayed for hours to consecrate the new nation to the God of all creation.

Washington's prayer for the United States of America appears on a plaque in Saint Paul's Chapel, as well as at Pohick Church, Fairfax County, Virginia, where Washington was a vestryman from 1762 to 1784. It reads:

Almighty God,

We make our earnest prayer that Thou wilt keep the United States in Thy Holy protection; and Thou wilt incline the hearts of the Citizens to cultivate a spirit of subordination and obedience to Government; and entertain a brotherly affection and love for one another and for their fellow Citizens of the United States at large, and particularly for their brethren who have served in the Field.

And finally that Thou wilt most graciously be pleased to dispose us all to do justice, to love mercy, and to demean ourselves with that Charity, humility, and pacific temper of mind which were the Characteristics of the Divine Author of our blessed Religion, and without a humble imitation of whose example in these things we can never hope to be a happy nation. Grant our supplication, we beseech Thee, through Jesus Christ our Lord. Amen.[15]

—GEORGE WASHINGTON

No one, unless they are a Christian, can make such a prayer to the God of heaven. Oh, yes, I will agree that they may pray, but in a perfunctory manner—not in this manner, and not with this conviction of heart. Washington's prayer was one of deep conviction in the providence of almighty God, calling upon the name above all names, whereby such a prayer would be honored by the eternal Father receiving it from the heart.

No one, whether he or she claims belief in Jesus or not, can readily and with conviction and full cognizance of what he or she is saying call Jesus *Lord* unless they have the Holy Spirit of God, according to Scripture (1 Cor. 12:3).

Unless a person is born again, he cannot enter or be aware of the kingdom of God (John 3:3–8), and therefore a person's public statements and behavior will mirror his private convictions, because men speak out of what is in their hearts (Matt. 15:18; Mark 7:21; Luke 6:45), and that is where the Lord looks. Man's tendency is to look at a person's public affiliations, pedigree, church attendance, or whether or not they take Communion—in other words, the outward trappings and appearances. But although "man looks at the outward appearance…the LORD looks at the heart" (1 Sam. 16:7).

At the same time, it must be noted that what *The Harbinger* reveals concerning the seminal day of the American nation-state in no way depends on what was going on in the heart of Washington or any other. Rather, it concerns the words and actions spoken. The Bible itself gives examples of prophetic words being spoken by people with ungodly motives or simply by those who spoke without realizing what they were saying. This is interesting, since *The Harbinger* shows the parallel between George Washington and King Solomon. King Solomon is one whom the Bible records as going after foreign gods—yet in no way did that invalidate his building of the temple or the sacred convocation and dedication over which he presided. Nor does it in the least diminish the power of the inspired writings of his included in the cannon of the Bible. The same exact principle underlies what is revealed concerning America's inaugural day.

America and the Consecration Ground

We follow now the narrative in *The Harbinger* where Nouriel Kaplan and the prophet are discussing the founding of America and the unique way it became a free and independent nation. We go to the chapter titled "The Mystery Ground," where we pick up their conversation:

> [The prophet] took me around the corner and down the street. There was a statue in the distance. "Do you recognize him?" he asked.
>
> "Washington?"
>
> "Correct."
>
> It was a dark bronze statue of George Washington that stands on Wall Street facing the New York Stock Exchange. We drew nearer, coming to a stop just short of the platform on which it rested. From there we gazed up at the dark stoic figure.
>
> "My dream!" I said. "This is exactly how he looked in my dream. He wasn't as big, but I was looking up at him the same way...from the same angle. And his right hand was extended just like that."
>
> "And turned downward just like that," he said, "to rest on the Bible....
>
> "This is where it all began. This is where the United States of America, as we know it, came into existence."

"In New York City."

"In New York City…and here."

"Here?"

"Here," he replied, "as in *right* here. There's an inscription on the pedestal. Read it, Nouriel. Read it out loud."

So I did:

On this site in Federal Hall, April 30, 1789 George Washington took the Oath as the First President of the United States of America.

"*On this site*…I've seen this statue so many times and never stopped to think about why it was here."

"Here is where it all happened: April 30, 1789, the streets and rooftops are overflowing with people. Washington places his hand on the Bible and swears the oath. The crowd breaks out in cheers, cannons boom, and bells ring across the city. Then he withdraws into Federal Hall where he delivers the first presidential address before Congress. After that, he leads the nation's first government on foot in procession to the little stone sanctuary to commit the nation's future in prayer to God."

"Where?" I asked.

"That's the key," he replied.

"The key to the mystery?" I asked.

"Yes."

"It would be the ground on which the nation was committed to God, the nation's ground of consecration."…

"Come, Nouriel," he said. "It's time to see the place where it all happened…America's ground of consecration. Let's follow their steps as the president led them through the streets of the city on foot to the appointed place. Let's go."

So we walked down Wall Street and then onto another. I could picture it all as it happened two centuries earlier: Washington, the first senators, the first representatives, the first cabinet, America's first government, all heading to the sacred gathering. But it was now just me and the prophet, retracing the journey.... "There it is, Nouriel," he said, pointing to a building across the street. "There it is. The place where America was dedicated to God."

The place was surrounded by a dark wrought-iron fence.

"Is that the same little stone church?"

"Yes," he answered.

The building was distinctive looking and yet, at the same time, in view of what it represented, inconspicuous. In the front was a columned, classical-looking façade. In the back was a steeple, tall, narrow, and more what you'd expect to find in an old church building.

"You might not even notice it," I said.

"What you're looking at, Nouriel, is St. Paul's Chapel. It stands now much as it did on April 30, 1789, when America's first government entered through its doors. It was here that the nation's first president, Senate, and House of Representatives bowed together in prayer to consecrate the new nation's future into the hands of God. This is the place where the new nation was committed to the Almighty: this is America's ground of consecration."...

"America," he said, "was committed to God at the corner of what would become Ground

Zero. It was here, at Ground Zero, that they all gathered—George Washington, John Adams, America's Founding Fathers. They all came to the corner of Ground Zero to pray on the day that America's foundation was laid…as the consecrating act of that foundation. It was here that they came to commit the nation's future to God's *holy protection*. And it was here where that holy protection would be withdrawn."[16]

America may have declared its independence from Great Britain by rebellion and revolution, but once it had fought and won it by blood, its new leaders established it by prayer and supplication at Ground Zero—its ground of consecration inside St. Paul's Chapel—before God.

America's very first act as a nation was a prayer of dedication to almighty God, made by its founders, to petition Him for His protection and blessings over the new nation. Now, who can say definitively that God would not answer such a prayer? Who would dare to do so, especially in light of how greatly the Lord has blessed this nation? The evidence speaks volumes for itself. To speak against it is a fool's errand.

What *The Harbinger* Says About Covenants

When a critic of *The Harbinger* posits that there is no indication in Scripture that a Gentile nation can enter into a covenant with God, he is absolutely correct—if the covenant in question is unilateral.

Once again, no one is arguing that point or making that claim, and neither does *The Harbinger*. Neither is anyone making the claim that the prayer offered by our founders to God was a covenant along the lines of those that God established unilaterally, like the Abrahamic covenant and the new covenant.

What *The Harbinger* does say is that those who founded the American civilization saw themselves in covenant with God. They literally spoke of having entered into covenant with Him.

One critic has claimed this is *replacement theology*. No—it's called history, American History 101. It's a fact that can't be argued away. *The Harbinger*'s statement is historical.

Replacement Theology?

Let me pause for a couple of paragraphs to address the charge of replacement theology. How could Jonathan Cahn possibly believe in replacement theology? As a Jewish believer, he would have to replace himself...with himself! The congregation he leads is called Beth Israel. His ministry headquarters is called the Jerusalem Center. He preaches against replacement theology all the time. This charge, and the fact that others have sought to use it, gives the reader a little example of just how baseless the attacks against *The Harbinger* have been.

One critic claimed that since *The Harbinger* speaks of the destruction of ancient Israel, it must mean that Jonathan Cahn is saying God is finished with Israel. By that logic, since the Books of Kings and Chronicles speak about the destruction of Israel, the northern kingdom, then the Bible must be into replacement theology too! The Bible isn't, and neither is *The Harbinger*.

Getting Back to the Covenants

The Harbinger also notes that America's initial
Puritan founders did emphatically believe that
America was in covenant with God and that they
did establish and consecrate America to God on
that basis. *The Harbinger* notes that America was
conceived and dedicated to God's purposes at its
foundation. One critic used this to insist that this
clearly means America is in covenant with God.
Really? If one dedicates one's car to God and to
the fulfilling of God's purposes, does that mean
one's car is now in covenant with God?

Whether or not God honored this covenanting
of the founders of America is a question left open
to discussion. But the fact is, the civilization they
founded has become the most prosperous, powerful, and blessed nation in modern times.

Dr. Jacob Prasch has observed the following:

> This nation [the United States] is like Israel. There
> are five countries in human history…five…that
> have had more biblical influence than any other in
> their foundations as societies and nations—Israel,
> Great Britain, the United States, New Zealand,
> and South Africa. No five countries in human
> history have had as much influence of the Scrip-
> tures in their foundations as nations and societies
> as Israel, Great Britain, America, South Africa,
> and New Zealand.[17]

This is an unquestionable historical fact that
carries with it great import to the founding of
this republic. It places it in a very special place
in comparison with Israel. Israel was founded by

covenant, and the United States of America was founded by prayer within the grace of almighty God and His providence.

What's more, God, who is sovereign over all nations (Ps. 22:26–31), has promised to bless those nations who bless His people—the Jewish people (Gen. 12:3)—and no nation under heaven or in history has ever been as much a haven and a refuge for more of God's people as has the United States.[18]

It is the new covenant and faith in Jesus that predicates the belief that any person or group of people can pray to God in the name of Jesus and expect their prayers to be heard and honored by God. Because of this, any person or group of people representing any nation on the face of the earth can, as its leaders, pray to God for His blessings and protection and expect that prayer to be answered. A god who would not honor such prayers is not the God of the Bible, for He pleads for all people and nations to come to Him, that they may live (Isa. 45:20, 22; 55:3; Amos 5:1, 4, 6; Acts 10:34–35; 14:16; 15:6–11; 17:30–31; Eph. 6:1–3; 1 Tim. 2:4; Titus 2:11.).

By invoking the name of Jesus and calling upon the God of heaven in solemn prayer, a nation's leaders petition the Almighty to establish for themselves, and for their nation and posterity, the blessings extended by grace through faith in that name and the promises that anyone who calls upon that name shall most assuredly be delivered and saved.

Chapter 10

ISRAEL and AMERICA: UNIQUE AMONG NATIONS

A VERY GOOD POINT that a relative of mine who leans toward Reformed theology made about Israel's unique status is that the people of Israel—the Jewish people—are the nation, and the nation is the Jewish people. It is a valid one.

He pointed out that this distinction is unique to Israel alone and no other nation; therefore, no other nation can make that claim. Israel, as a nation, is uniquely identified with its population— the Jewish people. If there were no Jews in the world today, there would be no Israel. The modern state of Israel would not exist. Good point— in fact, an excellent one.

The Narrative of Israel

Israel was founded by a unilateral covenant God made with one man—Abram—and one woman— Sarai—when He brought them out of Ur of the Chaldeans in Mesopotamia. He brought them to a land He promised to them and to their descendants through their son, Isaac. The covenant God made with Abram was inextricably connected to the land He promised to him and tied to his descendants through Isaac (Gen. 17:19, 21).

This was known as the Abrahamic covenant (Gen. 12:1–3).

God gave Abram and Sarai new names—Abraham and Sarah—because one of the promises He made to them was that He would make them the parents of many nations and that through them all of the nations of the earth would be blessed. He also promised Sarah that nations and kings would be born from her (Gen. 17:6).

Abraham had two children: Ishmael, through Hagar, Sarah's Egyptian servant (Gen. 16);[1] and later Isaac, whom Sarah birthed at an advanced age. But it was through Isaac, and later Isaac's son Jacob (whom God renamed Israel), that God founded that mighty nation through whom He would bless all of the families of the earth, as the Messiah would come forth from it, and He would be the salvation of the human race and God's imputed righteousness to all who would believe. All of these promises came to pass.

The United States of America cannot make the claim that it can be identified with a distinct people, as Israel can, nor can it make the claim that it was founded by a unilateral covenant between God and one man, from which America's people emerged as a distinct nation, because that never happened. These claims are distinct to the Jewish people who have historically constituted the nation of Israel and today comprise the modern state of Israel. The Jewish people and Israel are one and the same.

Even with the Jewish people's two-thousand-year exile and scattering among the nations, and even with their regathering from all those lands where God had scattered them, Israel is the one distinct nation in the land God promised to Abraham, Isaac, and Jacob. Every one of the people who've returned to the land is a Jew regardless of his or her place of birth. The people are distinctly the nation, and the nation is distinctly its people.

Therefore, regardless of the land of origin any Jew hails from, wherever he chooses to go and make his home, he remains a Jew. This is his birthright; this is his legacy; this is his covenant with his God. No nation except Israel can make that claim.

What's more, the people of Israel and the nation they comprise are inextricably and unilaterally tied by covenant with God to the land He promised them—so it can also be said that Israel is the land and the people of the land are the Jewish people. No other nation can make that claim, either.

Though no other nation can claim that its land was promised to it by God, the Scriptures do teach that He has set the boundaries of all people and nations (Gen. 11:7–9; Deut. 32:8; Acts 17:26).

With regard to the United States, America is not comprised of a distinct people like Israel is. Unlike Israel, America is not the people, nor is it the land, and it was not founded by unilateral covenant with God, as Israel was.

The America-Israel Connection

But America *was* colonized by people of devout faith in God, who came to these shores and

settled this land and consecrated it and themselves for the propagation of the gospel of peace—
the gospel of Israel's Messiah. Many of them came
here envisioning themselves as a new Israel entering a new promised land, dedicating themselves
to bringing the faith in the one true God to its
natives—to conquer them, as it were, with this
faith, just as ancient Israel conquered Canaan and
brought faith in the one true God to the land.

I think it bears repeating that the first act of
this fledgling nation's leaders—a joint session of
Congress led by its first president—was to consecrate by prayer the United States of America—
its people and its land—to almighty God in the
name of Jesus. They did this at a small church on
the corner of what today is called Ground Zero, at
a place called St. Paul's Chapel in New York City,
the nation's capital at the time.

As I stated earlier, according to Dr. Jacob
Prasch, there have only been five nations in history founded like Israel with such strong biblical
roots—Great Britain, Australia, New Zealand,
South Africa, and the United States. According
to him, all of these nations, including Israel, have
backslidden and are today in an advanced degen-
erative state.[2]

Among these nations, the United States stands
out because it was established by a bilateral covenant of its founders through the consecration
of their prayers in St. Paul's Chapel to God "for
His blessings, and His protection." Let us speak
of this.

It is this first act of consecrating the new

nation to God on April 30, 1789, by a joint session
of Congress and the president that established
the United States of America as a nation consecrated and dedicated to God. No other act in this
nation's history (with the exception of President
Abraham Lincoln's creation of a National Day of
Prayer) would ever be so significant for its destiny
since its founding.

Apart from America, no other nation but Israel
has had as the act of its first leaders a convocation to prayer to petition God for its protection
and blessing. America stands unique with Israel
among the nations of the earth in this respect. No
other nation has ever been founded on the prayers
of its first leaders other than the United States of
America and Israel.

Another similarity that both nations have in
common is that they are comprised of exiles and
refugees from foreign lands. Even upon entering
Canaan, Israel was a refugee people, fleeing slav-
ery in Egypt en route to a land promised to them
by God's Abrahamic covenant, though it was a
homogeneous population at the time.

Today, the United States of America, like the
modern state of Israel, is comprised of popula-
tions from every nation under heaven, with many
languages, though its people mostly speak its predominant language, which is English. It is a land
of exiles[3] and refugees. And it is to the land and
the nation established on it where these diverse
people from many lands have come to make their
home. It is here where they choose to become its
citizens.

The United States of America has become a microcosm of the human race, containing people from every nation under heaven. The modern state of Israel is smaller, but it too is a very similar microcosm of every nation under heaven, inasmuch as the Jewish people who've returned and resettled its land come from every nation under heaven.

Today, America is comprised of people with different cultural roots and customs, yet it contains a predominantly distinctive American culture into which all of these people assimilate. Modern Israel is comprised of a people reflecting many cultures and languages, yet its predominant culture is distinctly Jewish and its predominant faith is Judaism.

Israel has been blessed and protected by God from its enemies, and its land today yields abundant crops of every variety, making it one of the chief exporters of produce in the world. America, likewise, has been blessed of the Lord and protected by God from its enemies, and its land today yields abundant harvests, much of which it exports to other nations, making it the leading exporter of produce in the world today.

These are the differences and similarities between Israel and America. Both are and have been a refuge for the largest concentration of God's chosen people in history, and both have been blessed by God and protected as no other nation in history. This is a fact of history and an act of God. To deny it or explain it away is to deny the hand of almighty God in human history.

America is more than its people; it is an answer to prayer—the prayer of consecration that its founders made to the God of all creation, the God of the Bible, who lives, hears, and answers such prayers when made by leaders of nations who honor Him and acknowledge His hand in human history, as Nebuchadnezzar personally discovered (Isa. 56:3, 6–8).

Chapter 11

The TRUE AMERICA-ISRAEL CONNECTION

THE PRAYERS OF America's founders, including those of George Washington as general of the Colonial Army and later as the new nation's president (which all of those who were in attendance also concurred in silent consent), are criticized by some because Washington was a Gentile praying for a nation with whom God had not covenanted. However, these prayers of America's founders stand as examples of the prayers of Gentiles throughout history, including biblical prayers by Gentiles who called upon the name of almighty God in their time of need, fully anticipating that not only would God hear their prayers, but He would answer them as well.

Prayers of Gentile People

We will consider some of these prayers from Gentiles, beginning with the prayer and supplication of a biblical people who were not in covenant relationship with God and who were not Israelites—the ancient Assyrian people of the city of Nineveh.

The Assyrians of Nineveh

In the Book of Jonah, we see God calling Jonah
(His Hebrew prophet) to prophesy to a non-
Jewish city (Nineveh) with a population that neither has a covenant relationship with God nor
established God as its god. Yet when everyone
in it heeds Jonah's message, repents before the
God of heaven, and prays to Him as a people, He
relents and does not destroy them. Repentance
requires prayer, and Scripture substantiates that
God heard the prayers of repentance offered to
Him by these Gentile pagans.

Ironically, if the letter of the Law was applied,
Jonah—who prophesied of impending judgment
and destruction for Nineveh—would have been
stoned under that Law for prophesying something
that didn't come to pass: the city's destruction in
three days. This serves as a good example that the
letter kills, as the apostle Paul has made clear, but
the Spirit imparts life (2 Cor. 3:6).[1]

The critics forget the myriad prayers of people
who predated Abram who called upon the name
of the Lord (Gen. 4:26); also, we know that before
the Flood, people like Enoch and Noah "walked
with God" (Gen. 5:24; 6:9); lastly, a good many
who postdated Abraham and prayed to the God
of heaven were heard and answered by God, such
as Ruth the Moabitess, whom the Hebrew Bible
honors with Israel, the people of God (Ruth
1:14–18; 3:1–18; 4:7–21).

Ebed-Melech, the Ethiopian

Nebuchadnezzar went up against Jerusalem to take it by storm, taking the city and all of the rulers of Judah captive and slaying them, including the killing of King Hezekiah's sons right before his eyes.

But God protected Ebed-Melech, the Ethiopian, and spared his life while the armies of the Chaldeans captured and plundered Jerusalem and killed its people. Even the ones whose lives were spared were exiled to Babylon. However, God delivered this foreigner on that day, saying, "'Because you have trusted in Me,' declares the LORD" (Jer. 39:18). This example reveals the critical importance of remembering God's point of view: "God sees not as man sees, for man looks at the outward appearance, but the LORD looks at the heart" (1 Sam. 16:7).

How is it that this one foreigner who lived in the midst of Israel found grace, while all of Israel's leaders were either led into captivity or died by the sword? He trusted and called upon the name of the Lord, and they did not (Jer. 39:15–18). This was a man who understood what God spoke through the mouth of the psalmist when He promised everyone:

> Call upon Me in the day of trouble;
> I shall rescue you, and you will honor Me.
> —PSALM 50:15

More examples from the history of other righteous Gentiles who are honored in Scripture can be cited, but the ones we've cited here will suffice for now. Without question, I posit to all thinking Christians here, basing what I write upon the clear teachings of the Holy Scriptures, that God hears the prayers of all people and all nations. Not only is this biblical, but it is found from Genesis to Revelation.

New Testament Gentiles

There are others in the New Testament who, as Gentiles, prayed to the God of heaven in the name of Jesus. We cannot dismiss their prayers because they were not of the natural seed of Abraham with whom God had made His exclusive covenant. God's purpose in establishing this unique unilateral covenant with Abraham was to bless all of the nations of the earth through him, as the Scriptures say (Gen. 18:18).

Indeed, it can be argued that God answers the prayers of people who are not Christians and those of non-Jews—people and nations that have not historically had a covenant relationship with the God of Israel and who were not partakers of the Abrahamic covenant at its inception when God made His promises to Abraham.

The entire Hebrew Bible contains other examples of Gentiles whom God healed. The Lord Jesus Himself made this point when He taught at the synagogue of Nazareth (Luke 4:25–27). But God has broken down the barrier of the dividing wall, which is the Law of commandments ratified in the Mosaic covenant, and He has done this through the death of Jesus once and for all, with no distinctions other than to accept Jesus as Lord and Savior in faith and be born of the Holy Spirit of God and washed in the cleansing blood of Jesus.

God's Works and Acts Among the Gentile Nations

Out of two, God has created one new man, and out of the nations, He has brought forth children unto Himself, whom He has incorporated into His people, Israel, as one people with one faith, one hope of our calling, one Lord, one God— our Lord Jesus who is Lord above all and over all, amen (Isa. 56:3, 6, 8; Zech. 14:9; John 10:16; 11:52; 1 Cor. 8:6; Eph. 4:4).

God's plan of redemption does not originate in the covenants, but the covenants originate in it—within the framework of God's redemptive plan, which He established long before He made these covenants with man, long before He laid the world's foundation.

In the providence of God, the totality of God's redemptive plan must be taken into consideration, not subdivided and layered with theological limitations of what God can accomplish throughout history, as though these limits imposed on Him by the minds of men will keep Him from His purpose.

We must never forget that the prayers of those who are Gentile Christians, having received Jesus by faith as Lord and Savior, having been born again of the Holy Spirit of God, are heard and answered. Gentiles have received of the grace of God to the nations, and by faith they have been inducted through Jesus into this nation with

whom God established His covenant—the Abrahamic covenant.

It is through Jesus that the promises made to
Abraham[2] have been extended to all who come
by faith through Him to God from every nation
under heaven. It is not necessary for Gentiles to
become Jews through the *bris* of circumcision
according to the Law (read Paul's letter to the
Galatians). There is no exception, and anyone who
attempts to make one is guilty of trying to rees-
tablish one where God in Jesus has abolished it.

The Abrahamic covenant is only exclusive to the
land and its people—the Jewish people. The promise of blessing to the nations extends through Jesus
in what Paul calls "the mystery" of the promise of
God (Col. 4:3). This blessing provides the way for
the nations of the world to become fellow heirs—
wild olives grafted into God's olive tree Israel—and
to be made partakers with Israel of the promises
He made to Abraham through faith—faith in Jesus.

Under the inspiration of the Holy Spirit and
the foreknowledge of almighty God, Paul writes
of the one people of God comprising God's olive
tree, of grafted wild olives—Gentiles—and
regrafted Jewish believers in Jesus the Messiah—
national Israel and His remnant of Jews and Gentiles (Eph. 2:11–22).

Indeed, the God of Israel, when speaking to
the prophet Jeremiah, refers to Himself as "the
God of all flesh" (Jer. 32:37). Paul, in the Holy
Spirit, refers to God as the God of the Gentiles as
well (Rom. 3:29–31). Paul calls the Gentiles "fellow heirs and fellow members" (Eph. 3:6).

The premise that God's standards change from nation to nation and that His Word does not apply outside of Israel, because Gentiles are not a part of God's covenant people (I agree to a point—outside of Jesus, they are not), is both unbiblical and ludicrous, because there is ample evidence of God dealing with Gentile nations and Gentile people long before He made His covenant with Abraham and long after He made it. God will continue to deal with people in this way until the day Jesus returns. The grace of almighty God to all people who call upon His name can be discovered in His Word from Genesis to Revelation.

Daniel's Vision

When Daniel sees his vision of God's throne and gazes upon the coming of the Son of Man, the Messiah, approaching the Ancient of Days, he is given the following description of the extent of the kingdom this Son of Man will be king over:

> I kept looking in the night visions,
> And behold, with the clouds of heaven
> One like a Son of Man was coming,
> And He came up to the Ancient of Days
> And was presented before Him.
> And to Him was given dominion,
> Glory and a kingdom,
> That all the peoples, nations and men of every
>   language
> Might serve Him.
> His dominion is an everlasting dominion
> Which will not pass away;

And His kingdom is one
Which will not be destroyed.
—DANIEL 7:13–14

The description is one that encompasses all nations and men of every language on the face of the earth. And as for His kingdom, it is prophesied that it will not be destroyed or pass away. This kingdom will contain within its domain all of the nations of the earth.

This will not be a man-made new world order devoid of nations and led by unscrupulous globalists paid by central bankers and elitists, but rather a Messianic millennial kingdom comprised of all the nations of the earth with God at its head and His Messianic King on the throne of David, being one of his descendants.

Take note: There is no indication in the prophecy that any of the nations will be absorbed into a single collective, as has been attempted by man without the agency of God since the Tower of Babel. Rather, the indication is that it will be comprised of the nations of all the earth.

What does this indicate? What does it entail regarding the Abrahamic covenant? It is its fulfillment, where God has said that all of the nations of the earth would someday be blessed through Abraham's descendant. How will they be blessed? By being included through the Messiah in the commonwealth of God as His people.

Conclusion: God's Promise to All
Nations Includes Israel

Herein lies the message and warning of *The Harbinger*. God's people in America are that remnant of believers—Jews and Gentiles—from among the nations who dwell in this land and call upon the name of the Lord, who have made their peace with God through the sacrifice of the cross of Jesus—Israel's Messiah—for their redemption (Isa. 53:10–11; Ps. 50:5; Rom. 3:25; 5:9; Eph. 1:7; Col. 1:20; Heb. 9:12; 13:12) and who now must call upon that blessed name (Joel 2:32; Acts 2:21; 4:12; Rom. 10:13) for this nation in order to avert the disaster and calamity that will befall it if we do not heed the warning of the nine harbingers that have been placed before us. To that end, *The Harbinger* has been written to sound that warning as the sound of a trumpet blast across America in a call to repent, to return, and to recall the good things the Lord has done, which He wishes for us once again, if we but turn to Him and seek His face as His people should. The Lord Himself has declared:

> "Then if they will really learn the ways of My people, to swear by My name, 'As the LORD lives,' even as they taught My people to swear by Baal, they will be built up in the midst of My people. But if they will not listen, then I will uproot that nation, uproot and destroy it," declares the LORD.
>
> —JEREMIAH 12:16–17

We do well to heed this warning as given in the scripture above. It is the warning of the Lord God, the Almighty Himself, and it pertains to the nations who have learned the ways of God and call upon His name, who have partaken of the blessings of Abraham through Jesus.

Do I doubt that the Lord Himself is speaking through His watchmen in this hour—watchmen such as Jonathan Cahn and many others? Absolutely not, for Scripture itself bears witness without doubt that God's servants are given utterance to speak in His name the things of God to succeeding generations, and thus the gospel is spread from land to land and people to people—and with it, a call to repent. Wake up!

America's Moral Descent

On December 7, 1993, William J. Bennett delivered a speech at the Heritage Foundation in Washington DC, where he described just how far the country had degenerated in the previous thirty years.

Using a statistical measure and beginning from 1960, Bennett said that since that time, the gross domestic product had nearly tripled, violent crime had increased at least 560 percent, divorces had more than doubled, the percentage of single-parent homes had tripled, and, by the end of the decade, 40 percent of all American births and 80 percent of minority births had occurred out of wedlock.[3]

Bennett compared the top problems in American schools of the 1940s—talking out of turn, gum-chewing, making noise, and running in the hall—to those of 1990, which had gravitated to drugs, alcohol consumption, pregnancy, suicide, rape, and assault and battery.

Dr. Bennett said, and I quote in part:

> There is a coarseness, a callousness and a cynicism to our era. The worst of it has to do with our children....People are losing their capacity for shock, disgust and outrage.[4]

Sound familiar? He continued by describing the spiritual state of our nation in this way:

> The ancients called our problem acedia, an aversion to spiritual things and an undue concern for the external and the worldly. Acedia also is the seventh capital sin—sloth—but it does not mean mere laziness. The slothful heart is steeped in the worldly and carnal, hates the spiritual and wants to be free of its demands.[5]

The Harbinger presents a very central and strong biblical message: that America's blessings come from God. It also presents the message that, just as was said in the prophetic warning made by its first president, if America departs from God, those blessings cannot ultimately be sustained.

America has broken that moral code many times over, and we stand today at the precipice of God's judgment, not because we broke any unilateral covenant with God—that is impossible for us to do under grace, just as it is impossible for Israel to do—but because we have transgressed His commandments. It is the transgression of those commandments that brings judgment to a nation.

And unless we turn, it will bring more chastening upon our nation—chastening upon repeated chastening—until a day dawns that, after repeatedly ignored warnings given by God, His judgment will strike our land as it did in ancient Israel and later Judah—and as it did in measure here on September 11, 2001.

Chapter 12

MYSTICISM, DREAMS, KABBALAH, and the ENLIGHTENMENT

T HE FINAL CONVERSATION that takes place in *The Harbinger* reveals the critically important responsibility the prophet was impressing upon Nouriel. It's a message not only for Nouriel but also for every person who has called upon the name of the Lord and has become a part of God's family:

"So, Nouriel, a question: Should the watchman refrain from reaching for his trumpet because people will find it disturbing and would rather hear a pleasant sound? Or should he refuse to blow it because they'll oppose and slander him or because they'll even hate him?"

"No," I replied.

"If the watchman should see the signs of calamity appearing in the distance and fail to blow the trumpet to warn his people, what then would he become?"

"Guilty."

"Of what?"

"Of their destruction."...

"[You're] a watchman on the wall who has seen the signs....And the city sleeps...the people have no idea what's coming....And to you is entrusted the sound of their awakening…and their redemption."[1]

Since the book was first released, it has made a lasting impact on those who have read it. Millions of people's lives have been impacted in a positive way by the message of *The Harbinger*. It has truly caused the Word to go forth and have its way with all those who have ears to hear it. It contains a life-changing message, and many have been saved and have joined the family of God as a result of reading it.

But just as is true with any message—including the message of Jesus in the Word of God—there have been some, albeit a very small number of people, who have come against it.

In this chapter we will deal with more of the attacks thrown at *The Harbinger*. As you will see, all of these criticisms are caused by mis-understanding or errant conclusions based on misinterpretation.

Mystery as a Four-Letter Word

Some critics have accused *The Harbinger* of being linked to mysticism. What is this based on? The fact that *The Harbinger* uses the word *mystery*. Apparently, in those critics' eyes, the word *mystery* is a dirty word or something short of theological profanity.

Why would a believer see the word *mystery* not as something to be delighted in, but as something to be shunned and opposed? If one constructs a very closed and narrow view of God, then there will be very little room or openness given to anything not already known. If one believes that one already knows everything there is to be known about God and His ways or everything that can be known, then one will see mysteries as something bad. If one believes, as some of these critics do, that God can give no further revelation in any way, then one will also shun any semblance of mystery.

But is this anti-mystery view a biblical one? Absolutely not! If one comes against *The Harbinger* for using the word *mystery*, then one has to come against the apostle Paul and the Bible itself—for Paul not only uses the word *mystery* but also delights in it. Why is that? Because Paul delights in the knowledge of God and knows that God is a God of revelation. God reveals. One cannot reveal something except that this something had to be formerly unrevealed. That which is unrevealed is a mystery until the time of its revelation.

Obviously, those who read *The Harbinger* are coming to discover things they never knew before. In that sense, what was a mystery before is now being revealed. Is God mysterious? Of course He is—to those who don't already know everything there is about Him. By definition, there is no end to what we don't know about God, and by definition, those things we don't yet know are mysteries until we know them.

This is not to be confused with any notion of God not being finished with Scripture or of His giving us a revelation that replaces Scripture, contradicts Scripture, or stands on an equal plane with Scripture. But to say that God does not give His people insight or new understanding is completely unbiblical. The Bible promises that the Spirit of God will lead and teach His children of His truth (John 16:13). Any such teaching is a revealing. Any such leading is, in a sense, outside of the Bible. But does that make it extrabiblical? Only in the sense that it wasn't specifically found in the Bible, but it was clearly within the framework of biblical revelation.

Jonathan Cahn did not draw from extrabiblical, mystical writings as his sources for his book. He drew from only one source for spiritual truth—the Bible. He believes that only the Bible is the Word of God.

If God were to warn a nation of judgment and give people insight to understand what is happening—to discern the "signs of the times"—then, in some way, something is being revealed that wasn't revealed before and could be called a mystery. This would not be an extrabiblical revelation, in the sense of being outside of the parameters of Scripture, nor would it be the revealing of what ancient Scripture means. Rather, it is simply that God is warning a nation of judgment. Whether one calls this a mystery or not, it is nothing more or less than that.

Jumping the Trigger and Spiritual McCarthyism

Some have expressed their concern semantically with the use of words like *mystery, mysteries, secrets, prophetic,* and *inspired,* contending that these words contain meanings that Jonathan

Cahn did not give to them. What has become a downside of some modern discernment ministries is a reflexive response to trigger words. In other words, if you use words, as *The Harbinger* does, like *ancient, mystery, vow, sacred, ground, secret,* or *key,* you must be linked to the Masons, the gnostics, or other groups such as these. It's a kind of spiritual McCarthyism that looks for superficial evidence and then applies guilt by association.

The problem is that the word *ancient* is used in the Bible, along with the words *mystery, vow, sacred,* and *secret.* Yes, any word can and will be used for all sorts of purposes. It's called language. But to make an argument based on the fact that one has used words that are also used for other purposes and that also happen to be used in Scripture is ridiculous. Where does it end? With this logic, one could indict God on the charge of heresy. (It's already been done.)

The Gnosticism Charge

Before we move on, let me also clarify that *The Harbinger* does not present or support any gnostic beliefs. The gnostics believed in knowledge that was to be kept secret—that was meant to stay a mystery. The message of *The Harbinger* is precisely the opposite. God is the One who reveals mysteries. *The Harbinger* does likewise—it reveals mysteries. Jonathan is no more a gnostic than the apostle Paul was a gnostic—although both speak of mysteries.

If there are no mysteries, then we know everything there is to know. But we don't. And God, by

His Spirit, means to lead us into continual insight and show us things we don't yet know. That's the opposite of gnosticism.

The (Very Crazy) Kabbalah Charge

There have been claims that Cahn was influenced in his writings by ancient mystical teachings from the Middle Ages, writings asserted to be secret ancient writings or compilations of secret ancient writings. This Jewish mystical school of thought came to be known as Kabbalah, meaning, "to receive, to accept."

The accusation, made by a few, that *The Harbinger* has been influenced by mystical Jewish writings such as the Zohar represent some of the most extreme and bizarre opposition he has faced. It is an extreme false accusation. One of these accusations was based on the fact that Cahn quoted from rabbinical texts to show that the rabbis expounded on such things as Isaiah 53 being about the Messiah or God being three in one—even the truth of the Messiah dying for our sins. These things can be used to share the gospel and have been a standard method of apologetics and evangelism for ages.

Rabbinical writings, as well as other writings of all sorts, mystical or otherwise, have been quoted for ages in Bible commentaries, apologetics, and works like *The Life and Times of Jesus the Messiah*. The apostle Paul actually quoted from a pagan hymn to Zeus in order to share the truth of the gospel at Mars Hill. If we were to accuse Paul of being into Zeus worship or of being secretly pagan, we would need to repent of bearing false witness.

What *The Harbinger* is actually saying is very simple: God judges nations. God warns of judgment. God is able to warn a nation of judgment in a way that is consistent with that which is found in the Bible. And now the same biblical pattern, progression, and signs of national judgment that appeared in the last days of ancient Israel are now manifesting in America—and these signs are appearing in uncanny, eerily precise manifestations.

The Harbinger is not only revealing these biblical mysteries and connections, but also making a call for repentance, salvation, and revival.[2]

The Mysterious Seals

In the chapter in *The Harbinger* titled "The Mystery Ground," the prophet continues his lessons to Nouriel using ancient seals to enlighten him. Some critics have focused on the fact that these "mysterious seals" are mentioned to bring the accusation of occultism.

What the critic calls "mysterious seals" are nothing more than a fictional prop used by Cahn to help illustrate and move the narrative along as he develops the various components relative to those seals and what they represent: the nine harbingers.

There is absolutely no reason to tie these seals or any other of the various fictitious elements within the fictitious narrative to mean anything other than what the author makes plain within that narrative. Cahn incorporates the technique of mixing fact with fiction in his narrative. Isn't that what Jesus did by telling parables? And beyond that, the seals in the story happened to be *biblical* seals, the kind referred to in the Bible itself.

The history of the United States is one that is rich in the Scriptures, having been founded upon the moral precepts of a rich Judeo-Christian heritage no other nation under heaven but Israel has ever had. Our first leaders specifically made it the first act of our government, upon our nation's founding, to pray to the Lord God of Israel for His divine protection and blessing. The evidence is the history of God's faithful blessings over America.

As with all enterprises, not every one of our Founding Fathers was a Christian, but a good many of them were, and I do not believe there has been a single enterprise outside of the first Jewish believers who had seen the risen Savior and brought the news to their unbelieving kinsmen in the flesh where everyone was a Christian.

If for that reason anyone claims that because of this, our nation was not founded upon Judeo-Christian precepts, I would have them reexamine our history, the documents, letters, legislation, conduct, and confessions of the intrepid men and women who were so instrumental in crafting our laws and our Constitution, so they may see for themselves the body of evidence there is to support that the United States was, upon its founding, united as a Christian nation under the God of the Bible, with its first president and its first leaders having submitted to heaven the prayers for its welfare to the only One who could bestow His blessings from heaven in the name of Jesus, in whose name the first president of these United States prayed.

The Harbinger: Received in a Dream?

One critic implies that a dream mentioned in the narrative of the book suggests that Jonathan Cahn somehow received his revelations from a dream. This is one of several bizarre misinterpretations this critic makes about the book. It is totally false. The dream in the book is clearly part of the narrative of the characters, but it is not the reality of how Jonathan Cahn received the revelations for the book. In this case, the critic has focused inaccurately on some key words—specifically, *mysterious seals*—in an attempt to present *The Harbinger* as something it is not.

As far as God being able to speak through dreams, this is clearly spoken of in Scriptures:

> It will come about after this
> That I will pour out My Spirit on all mankind;
> And your sons and daughters will prophesy,
> Your old men will dream dreams,
> Your young men will see visions.
> Even on the male and female servants,
> I will pour out My Spirit in those days.
> And they shall prophesy.
> I will display wonders in the sky and on the
> earth,
> Blood, fire and columns of smoke.
> The sun will be turned into darkness

And the moon into blood
Before the great and awesome day of the LORD
    comes.
And it will come about that whoever calls on
    the name of the LORD
Will be delivered.

—JOEL 2:28–32

Throughout the Scriptures, as early as Genesis, we see that God has often used dreams to communicate something extremely important that addresses a specific person or persons in a specific situation. This is the biblical manner and one of many ways that God uses to communicate with His servants.

We see this when Abraham and Sarah journeyed to Gerar, and there he presented himself and his wife as siblings to the ruler there. So Abimelech the king took Sarah as his wife. But that night:

God came to Abimelech in a dream of the night, and said to him, "Behold, you are a dead man because of the woman whom you have taken, for she is married." Now Abimelech had not come near her; and he said, "Lord, will You slay a nation, even though blameless? Did he not himself say to me, 'She is my sister'? And she herself said, 'He is my brother.' In the integrity of my heart and the innocence of my hands I have done this." Then God said to him in the dream, "Yes, I know that in the integrity of your heart you have done this, and I also kept you from sinning against Me; therefore I did not let you touch her. Now therefore, restore the man's wife, for he is

a prophet, and he will pray for you and you will
live. But if you do not restore her, know that you
shall surely die, you and all who are yours."

—GENESIS 20:3–7

Early the next morning Abimelech returned
Sarah to Abraham, having never touched her in
any way. Because Abimelech was a righteous and
God-fearing ruler, God spoke to him through a
dream and granted him grace through Abraham's
intercession on his behalf when he released and
returned Sarah back to Abraham (vv. 8–18).[3]

In the New Testament we see God using
dreams to communicate to His servants with
instructions about what they ought to do regarding a specific situation. For example, an angel of
the Lord appeared to Joseph in a dream to encour-
age him to marry Mary and to inform him that
the Child she was carrying was conceived of the
Holy Spirit (Matt. 1:18–25).

Later, we see Joseph warned in a dream:
"'Take the Child and His mother, and flee to
Egypt, and remain there until I tell you; for
Herod is going to search for the Child to destroy
Him.' So Joseph got up and took the Child and
His mother while it was still night, and left for
Egypt. He remained there until the death of
Herod" (Matt. 2:13–15).

The magi who came to see and worship the
Child were also warned in a dream about Herod
and his intentions, and they departed by another
route back to their lands without informing
Herod of their intentions (v. 12).

When it was time for Joseph and Mary to return with the Child to their land, an angel of the Lord spoke to Joseph in a dream and communicated such news to Joseph, and they returned to the land of Israel, though they did not go to Judea, because again Joseph was warned in a dream not to go there; so they settled in a city named Nazareth in the region of Galilee (vv. 19–23).

Even Pilate's wife dreamed about Jesus and exhorted Pilate not to have anything to do with that righteous Man (Matt. 27:19). In another example, God opened a door to Cornelius' salvation—a Roman centurion, no less—when He spoke to Peter in a trancelike dream (Acts 10:9–16).

There are many more examples from one end of the Scriptures to the other, demonstrating that God communicates through dreams and visions. God does not change, and His ways do not change. He has made it clear that this is what He is going to do in the last days.

Nevertheless, this is still beside the point, for to take the fact that a book mentions a dream in a story to mean that the book itself came from a dream—that is about as bad a hermeneutic (method of interpretation) as can be fathomed. It would be the equivalent of saying that since C. S. Lewis wrote a story of a talking lion, it follows that his book was actually dictated by that same talking lion! The absurdity of such an accusation (and of such logic) only goes to show how bizarre some of the charges hurled at *The Harbinger* have become. It is not to be unexpected. One cannot have a book of the nature, magnitude, scope, and impact of *The Harbinger* and avoid such controversy.

Chapter 13

The IMPORTANCE of GOOD DISCERNMENT

DISCERNMENT IS A good thing and a necessary part of our walk. The psalmist prayed, "Teach me good discernment and knowledge, for I believe in Your commandments" (Ps. 119:66). The simplest definition of *discernment* is "being able to choose correctly between right and wrong, truth and error." As believers in a dark world today, we need the Holy Spirit's gift of discernment.

The apostle Paul taught the Thessalonians to "examine everything carefully; hold fast to that which is good; abstain from every form of evil" (1 Thess. 5:21–22).

Good and Bad Discernment

Just as surely as good discernment is a necessary part of our walk, so too is bad discernment a hindrance to our Christian walk. In many cases, discernment has become something of a blank check by which some people have felt free to launch all kinds of public accusations against good men and women of God.

Jonathan Cahn, through *The Harbinger*, has learned how such things have hurt many good ministers and fellow believers. In spite of some hurtful so-called discernment aimed at *The Harbinger*, the Lord is fully in charge of it and has been from the beginning. The book has continued to go forth, to spread across the nation, to break records. Reports of repentance, revival, and salvation continue to flow in as a result of the spreading of the message of *The Harbinger*.

But it is a concern that the deterioration of godly discernment has affected some Christian brothers and sisters. We would hope—and pray—that in the end these sisters and brothers do not discover too late that the most dangerous forces threatening to bring about the demise of biblical discernment were to be found not from without the camp, but lurking within.[1]

Discernment is to be used by those who flow in the Holy Spirit of God. This is the reason it is so important first to be born again of the Spirit of God through Jesus and to read the Word of God with the guidance of the Holy Spirit. The Spirit of God will keep us from error and help the child of God to avoid mistreating and misreading theology into it (2 Pet. 1:20–21).

The Word of God, when read and studied properly with the Holy Spirit's guidance, brings to light God's message. The Holy Spirit always bears witness of Jesus (John 16:14) and glorifies Him (John 12:28) as the only way to God and gives Him preeminence in all things as King of kings and Lord of lords (John 14:6). He convicts the world of sin (John 16:8). He brings people to faith in God for redemption (John 6:44, 65). And He unlocks the teachings of the Bible (John 14:26;

16:13–15), which are a mystery to the unsaved. The Bible is nothing but a closed book that cannot be understood by the unregenerate mind, because its truths are spiritually discerned (1 Cor. 2:14).

One of the examples of inaccurate discernment that has been said about Jonathan Cahn since *The Harbinger* was first published is that he has claimed to be a prophet. He has never claimed to be a prophet and does not claim that his book is prophecy. Nor does the book offer an interpretation of Isaiah's prophecy. What it does do is describe a pattern that is being repeated in America that occurred in ancient Israel and which has been witnessed throughout history with great civilizations.

It lists nine warnings—nine harbingers—as they occurred. This is simply a matter of history. Because Cahn does not claim to be a prophet, the critic's misuse of Jeremiah 23:21 does not apply to the current situation. *The Harbinger* is a warning and a call to repentance, nothing more.

We Must Mature in Our Discernment

As believers, we need to understand how critically important it is to grow in our ability to correctly discern the truth from error. The writer of the letter to the Hebrews stressed this importance by saying, "Solid food is for the mature, who because of practice have their senses trained to discern good and evil" (Heb. 5:14). By taking a look at Daniel, who was able to correctly discern the meaning of a king's dream, we can better understand our need to be mature in our ability to discern.

King Nebuchadnezzar was subject to having dreams that left his spirit troubled and sleepless (Dan. 2:1). He called in all of his magicians, conjurers, sorcerers, and the Chaldeans to get the understanding for his dream. However, as many people do today, the king had forgotten what the dream was—he only knew it had left him disturbed and confused and anxious to know its meaning.

Nevertheless, he demanded, "If you do not make the dream known to me, there is only one decree for you!" (We can guess what this decree would be.) The Chaldeans answered the king by saying, "There is not a man on earth who could declare the matter for the king.... The thing which the king demands is difficult, and there is no one else who could declare it to the king except gods" (vv. 10–11).

Furious, the king sent out the decree that all the wise men should be slain—and Daniel and his friends were included in the search to be killed. But Daniel was a godly man; he spent time each day with his God, growing in wisdom and discernment between good and evil to help him face the difficulties of being held captive in a godless land. We read, "Then Daniel replied with discretion and discernment.... 'For what reason is the decree from the king so urgent?'" (vv. 14–15). When he learned what had happened with the king, Daniel asked for some time in order to be able to give the interpretation to him.

Daniel did what every godly man or woman seeking godly discernment should do: he went to his house, where God revealed the mystery to Daniel in a night vision. We know the rest of the story. Daniel gave the interpretation to the king—a dream so significant because it prophetically told of the future of the king's empire.

The Christian needs to be truly discerning, truly compassionate, truly unequivocating, and truly honest with the Lord and with himself and others in the body of the Lord. The apostle Paul prayed, "And this I pray, that your love may abound still more and more in real knowledge and all discernment, so that you may approve the things that are excellent, in order to be sincere and blameless until the day of Christ" (Phil. 1:9–10).

The Prophecy Within *The Harbinger* Concerning *The Harbinger*

The Lord Jesus taught that His message and those who would preach it without compromise would result in divisions among those who would hear it, because there would be those whom the Holy Spirit would disclose the message to and others who would reject the message given—for a myriad of reasons. For this reason, we need the witness of the Holy Spirit to confirm the word we hear. Without His witness, we will react from our own intellect in a form of spiritual blindness and cognitive dissonance that prevents us from "rightly dividing the word of truth" (2 Tim. 2:15, NKJV).

At the end of *The Harbinger* we read what appears to be a prophetic word concerning its reception by some and its rejection by others in the following dialogue between Nouriel Kaplan and the prophet:

> Then he [the prophet] stopped walking and turned around. "You're still concerned," he said, in a gentle voice.
>
> "The message," I said. "It's not the kind that wins popularity contests, is it?"
>
> "That would be a safe assumption."
>
> "They'll do everything they can to attack and discredit it."
>
> "Of course they will," he said. "Otherwise they'd have to accept it."
>
> "But not only the message."
>
> "No, the messenger as well."
>
> "They'll do everything they can to attack and discredit the one who bears the message."
>
> "Yes," said the prophet. "The messenger will be opposed, vilified and hated, mocked and slandered. It has to be that way, just as it was for Jeremiah and Baruch."[2]

Scriptural Examples of Opposition to God's Message and Moving

We read in the Scriptures that when Ezra and Nehemiah were rebuilding the temple and walls of Jerusalem, some of their enemies, hoping to hinder the work, offered to help with the rebuilding (Ezra 4:1–3). When this tactic didn't work, those who opposed the rebuilding tried another tactic. The Scriptures say:

> Then the people of the land discouraged the people of Judah, and frightened them from building, and hired counselors against them to frustrate their

counsel all the days of Cyrus king of Persia, even
until the reign of Darius king of Persia.

—Ezra 4:4-5

During the reign of Ahasuerus (Xerxes), they
banded together and organized in great numbers
to send a letter to the king, accusing the Jewish
people living in Jerusalem with being rebellious
and warning the king that if he were to allow the
rebuilding of Jerusalem, he would lose his posses-
sions beyond the river (vv. 8–16).

We read that when the work was approved,
each person had a specific assignment (Neh. 3)
and that even as the builders were doing the work,
they had to always be ready to fight. Some built
while others guarded with offensive weapons and
defensive armor in hand.

The rebuilders labored with one hand and had
a weapon in the other (Neh. 4:17–18). They were
all to listen for the trumpet blast so they could
rally and fight the battle together, but they relied
totally and completely on God for victory in the
battle. They never took off their "clothes" (perhaps
parallel to the armor of God) and always had their
swords in their hands (perhaps a connection to
the Word of God). The analogy is perfect.

The naysayers will always be around, just as
they were when Nehemiah set to rebuild the walls
of Jerusalem. Sanballat and Tobiah opposed them
continually and did everything humanly possible
to deter Nehemiah from his task and to keep him
from finishing the work the Lord put in his heart
to do.

So it was in the days of Ezra and Nehemiah, so it is now, and so it has always been. There has always been an organized religious opposition to God in every age. The first one was found in the Garden of Eden with the serpent. Since Adam and Eve had not yet conceived children, the enemy had to manifest himself in the form of one of the animals.

A method the Pharisees and Sadducees consistently and continuously used against the Lord Jesus was to bring their discourses against Him in public without His consent—not in private or in a setting where just they and He and His disciples could discuss their differences to resolve them.

These have been the methods used by those who opposed the Protestant Reformation and every group that has ever opposed God's movements in history. This is not the biblical method but the method used by the enemies of the gospel of our Lord and Savior, Jesus. Beware—you have been warned. Be truly discerning.

But God has always succeeded in accomplishing what He has set out to do, even with the enemy dragging his heels, kicking and screaming all along the way. This only serves to confirm that there is only one God, one Lord, and one King.

A Quick Look at the Bereans of the Bible

The Holy Scriptures are our template from which we derive our instruction as to how we should conduct ourselves among strangers and outsiders and among our community of believers, as well as how we ought to resolve our differences.

Some claim to be like the Bereans and call others to be like the Bereans as well—an excellent exhortation for all Christians to follow. But all one needs to do is read the Scriptures about the Bereans to see who they were. What does the Bible say? Let us go to it:

> The brethren immediately sent Paul and Silas away by night to Berea, and when they arrived, they went into the synagogue of the Jews. Now these were more noble-minded than those in Thessalonica, for they received the word with great eagerness, examining the Scriptures daily to see whether these things were so.
> —ACTS 17:10–11

We see here no evidence of anyone outing another Christian or other Christians or branding them as heretics over doctrinal matters. Rather, we see a group of believers engaged in a thorough examination of the claims of the gospel over the objections of those who opposed it.

Believers today, including those who have criticized *The Harbinger*, should apply this scripture to its proper context, because the Bereans searched the Scriptures for the gospel—they did not search the Scriptures to misapply them against other Christians with whom they disagree doctrinally. *This is a very big difference.*

Chapter 14

DOES *The HARBINGER* ADD to SCRIPTURE?

No, it does not. Several places in Scripture make allusion to other books that are not contained in our Bibles but that the scriptural record states unequivocally are just as authoritative historically, though not Scripture itself.

Such books as the Book of Jasher and certain books of the Apocrypha are used by some writers of the Bible, even though those books are not in the Word of God. In some cases, actual parts of the extrabiblical works are not only cited but also quoted by the writer, such as in the Book of Jude, where Jude quotes from the Ascension of Moses and applies it to what he writes in the Holy Spirit.[1] The Ascension of Moses was a Jewish work of the first century AD that presents a dispute that Michael the archangel had with the devil over Moses' remains. Then, in verses 14–15 of the Book of Jude, Jude quotes from another extrabiblical work—1 Enoch—and quotes directly from it to make his point. In doing this, Jude presents such works as authoritative enough to be included as examples to be cited, even within Scripture.

Now, no one is claiming the same for *The Harbinger*, but it should be argued that *The*

Harbinger is a book that calls Christians and the nation to repentance and to God, and as such should be heeded by every Bible-believing Christian and observant Jew. *The Harbinger* does not add another book to the canon of Scripture. It is not prophecy, but prophetic. A work can be prophetic without being prophecy, as the works cited by Jude in his brief letter show. While not prophecy, these works were used by the Holy Spirit in Jude's letter to speak prophetically to his generation and to all subsequent generations of believers.

This is what *The Harbinger* is. It is a prophetic warning, while not necessarily being prophecy, though it has been cited as prophecy by some.

As It Was in the Early Church, So It Is Today

The same controversy that has befallen the body of the Lord in the wake of the criticisms leveled against *The Harbinger* plagued the early church concerning its acceptance of Jude's letter.[2]

The Harbinger is not a work of eschatology, nor is it a an encyclopedic piece on end-time prophecy. Rather, it is simply a book that prophetically warns of impending judgments to follow if we as a nation do not turn to God. It presents the evidences of this judgment in the nine harbingers that have manifested themselves independent of and preceding the writing of the book. These nine harbingers, and everything related to them, are the warnings God has sent to this nation—to this generation—for it to heed and avert disaster.

Extra-Canonical Books Used by Old and New Testament Authors

Below is a list of extra-canonical books that are cited and in some cases quoted within the Hebrew Bible, also known as the Tanakh by Jews and called the Old Testament by Christians. These books are also called the protocanonical books:

- The Book of Jasher[3]
- The Book of the Wars of the Lord[4]
- A Book of Songs[5]
- The Chronicles of the Kings of Israel[6]
- The Book of Shemaiah the Prophet and Iddo the Seer[7]
- The Manner of the Kingdom[8]
- The Acts of Solomon[9]
- The Annals of King David[10]
- The Book of Samuel the Seer[11]
- The Book of Nathan the Prophet[12]
- The Book of Gad the Seer[13]
- The Prophecy of Ahijah[14]
- The Book of the Kings of Judah and Israel[15]
- The Book of Jehu[16]
- The Story of the Book of Kings[17]
- The Acts of Uzziah[18]
- The Vision of Isaiah[19]
- The Acts of the Kings of Israel[20]

+ The Sayings of the Seers[21]
+ The Laments for Josiah[22]
+ The Chronicles of King Ahasuerus[23]

We are warned not to add or remove a single prophecy from the Book of Revelation (Rev. 22:18), but the Bible does not speak against prophesying—otherwise the two witnesses in the Book of Revelation appearing in the last days (Rev. 11:3–13) would be both adding to God's written Word and considered false prophets for the act of prophesying.

What's the Purpose?

All of these things are for the glory of God, in order to affirm Him as Lord, and according to the Scriptures, the Holy Spirit convicts the world of sin, testifies of and glorifies Jesus, and teaches us all things as He opens the meanings of what we read in the Holy Scriptures.

We see also God's people stepping up in support of great ministries—the unseen people behind the scenes whom God has raised up to work the technical end of His message on radio and on television; the people whom God has called and raised up to keep our facilities clean; those who counsel to meet the distressed of God; those who are imparted to give an apt word at the right time by the Holy Spirit of God when it is needed.

When the Prophetic Is Not Prophecy

This is much like the prophetic word of Agabus in the Book of Acts, where prophets visited Antioch from Jerusalem, and one of them, named Agabus, prophesied that there would be a great famine in the land, which occurred during the reign of Claudius (Acts 11:27–30). We see here the need that presented itself and how God imparted a word of prophecy to meet that need before it transpired, helping the disciples prepare for it by taking collections for the brethren who lived in Judea, which Paul and his associates would bring to Jerusalem on their next trip there. Luke is careful to add that the need arose in the days when Claudius was emperor in Rome.[24]

Then we see the apostle Paul, while visiting the house of Philip the evangelist in Caesarea years later, meet the prophet Agabus again, whose visit coincided with his. Agabus had a specific word from the Holy Spirit for Paul about what awaited him, were he to travel to Jerusalem as he had planned. We see the prophet Agabus taking belts and binding himself in them, declaring that this will be the apostle's fate if he continues to the great and holy city (Acts 21:7–14). But Paul will not be dissuaded. He has made up his mind, and he will go to Jerusalem regardless of the peril that awaits him, because, as he says, "I am ready not only to be bound, but even to die at Jerusalem for the name of the Lord Jesus" (v. 13).

We saw in Agabus' prophetic words years earlier and now years later to Paul of specific prophetic warnings. We are not given the exact wording of the first one about the great famine that struck Judea during the reign of Claudius, but we are made known of the fact that it did come to pass in the reign of Claudius.[25]

Moreover, Luke mentions that Philip the evangelist had four virgin daughters who were prophetesses, but he does not include any of the prophecies or prophetic words these young women had ever uttered (Acts 21:9). The fact that they were prophetesses indicates there was occasion for them to have uttered something prophetically, but the Bible does not include it within the canon of Scripture; it just mentions that these women were virgins and that they were prophetesses.

There are also other examples of prophets prophesying, even King Saul prophesying along with the prophets when God chose him to be king over all Israel (1 Sam. 10:1, 17–25), but without giving us the details of what it was he or they prophesied (vv. 2–14).

These are but some examples of prophecies that never made it to the scriber's pen in the canon of the written Word of God—the Hebrew Scriptures—but whose stories serve as examples to us of the existence of such prophecies and prophetic words. These are not to be confused with the authoritative written canon of Scripture as embodied in the Old and New Testaments.

And herein is the problem.

The Broad Brushstroke of Cessationists

Cessationism claims that the working of the Holy Spirit as recorded in the Book of Acts came to an end at the time of the death of the apostles. Cessationists confuse modern prophetic utterances of the Holy Spirit as substitutes or additions to Scripture, rather than identifying them correctly with the types of prophecies the Scriptures mention but do not record, such as Agabus' first prophecy or those of Philip's daughters.

In the Hebrew Bible we read about the time when Israel asked for a king, and the Lord sent the prophet Samuel to anoint Israel's first king—Saul. This is perhaps the best-recorded example of the new birth and filling of the Holy Spirit we have in Scripture (prior to Pentecost), although it is not exclusive, since there are multiple examples of this in the prophets before the cross who spoke by the Word of God.

When Israel asked Samuel to petition God to appoint a king for them, he anointed Saul, whom God initially chose to be king over Israel. When they met, he gave Saul specific instructions:

> Come to the hill of God where the Philistine garrison is; and it shall be as soon as you have come there to the city, that you will meet a group of prophets coming down from the high place with harp, tambourine, flute, and a lyre before them, and they will be prophesying. Then the Spirit of the LORD will come upon you mightily, and you shall prophesy with them and be changed into another man. It shall be when these signs come to you, do for yourself what the occasion requires, for God is with you....
>
> Then it happened when he turned his back to leave Samuel, God changed his heart; and all those signs came about on that day. When they came to the hill there, behold, a group of

prophets met him; and the Spirit of God came
upon him mightily, so that he prophesied among
them. It came about, when all who knew him
previously saw that he prophesied now with the
prophets, that the people said to one another,
"What has happened to the son of Kish? Is Saul
also among the prophets?" A man there said,
"Now, who is their father?" Therefore it became
a proverb: "Is Saul also among the prophets?"
When he had finished prophesying, he came to
the high place.

—1 SAMUEL 10:5–7, 9–13

The Scriptures do not disclose what Saul
prophesied, and there is no record of what he said,
but the biblical text attests that Saul did prophesy that day.

Another place that records prophesying without disclosing the prophecies by unnamed
prophets is in the nineteenth chapter of the first
Book of Samuel. This was the period when Saul
began having murderous intent toward David and
was pursuing him. We read that when Saul discovered that David had fled from him to Naioth
at Ramah, he sent three companies of men to that
location to capture and bring David back to him in
chains (1 Sam. 19:1–20). However, each time one
of these three companies of men reached Samuel's
location where he and the company of prophets
were prophesying, the Spirit of God came upon
Saul's men, and they also prophesied (vv. 18–21).

The biblical record says that Saul decided to
proceed to Naioth in Ramah himself, and the
Spirit of God came upon him also and he too

prophesied. He also stripped off his clothes and lay down naked before Samuel, prophesying all that day and all that night. Therefore they said, "Is Saul also among the prophets?" (v. 24).

The sacred writings do not disclose to us what it was that these men were prophesying, but only mention the act. Yet the prophecies we are told about but do not read were as valid as those recorded in the sacred text itself, and equally as inspired, because the Scriptures say the Spirit of God came upon them and they prophesied (v. 20). Even Saul underwent this phenomenon, for the record says when he proceeded to go to Naioth in Ramah, the Spirit of God came upon him, so that he went along prophesying continually until he came to Naioth in Ramah (v. 23).

Such prophetic utterances and words of encouragement or warnings are given to specific people at specific times to meet the specific needs of circumstances pertaining only to them, yet these prophecies do not carry the authority and weight of Scripture.

Cessationists confuse these extrabiblical prophecies with the spoken prophecies that made it to the closed canon of Scripture and discount the existence of them, based on the false premise that because the writings of the two Testaments have been completed and gathered, there is no need for these sign gifts. There is not a single place in the Scriptures where this is taught or declared, but cessationists are so dogmatic, so spartan in their approach to biblical interpretation that they claim all such prophetic utterances undermine the concept of *Sola Scriptura*.

Cessationist Fallacies

This is an absolute cessationist fallacy—prophetic utterances do not undermine the concept of *Sola Scriptura*. We see prophetic utterances throughout Scripture, from the Hebrew Bible to the New Testament, and not once do any of the writings of Paul or any of the apostles or the teachings of our Lord Himself express the reservations expressed by cessationists.

To claim that such prophecies and the prophetic utterances connected to them pronounced but not recorded in the canon of Scripture undermine the Scriptures is a fulfillment of 2 Timothy 3:5, where Paul in the Holy Spirit prophesies of men in the last days who will have a form of godliness but will deny its power. Yes, cessationists have a "form of godliness"—a religious or spiritual, even theological air about them—but when pressed, they deny the power, or life, presumably within them (if the person is a born-again Christian)—what the Bible calls "Christ in you, the hope of glory" (Col. 1:27). This is how they do it: by denying that certain aspects of the work of that life within—what Paul calls "the law of the Spirit of life in Christ Jesus" (Rom. 8:2)[26]— no longer apply or are active. They deny the work and function of the Holy Spirit. But the Scriptures tell us that one and the same Spirit works *all* these things, distributing to each one individually, just as He wills (1 Cor. 12:11).

By denying any aspects of the work of the Holy Spirit's role essential for the work of service in Jesus, cessationists deny the reason for the Holy Spirit's advent following Messiah's ascension to the Father. In essence, they deny Jesus, for He is the One who wills and works in us for God's good pleasure through the Holy Spirit. Any expression or profession of faith that denies the work and ministry gifts of the Holy Spirit, with the exception of the office of apostleship,[27] denies Jesus, and this, John the evangelist warns, is the influence of an antichrist spirit, which is in the world and works to undermine the preaching of the gospel (John 8:43, 47; 1 Cor. 12:3; 14:32; 1 John 2:23; 4:1–6; 5:1, 7).

Christians who succumb to this influence through cessationist teachings are on one end of the theological spectrum. On the other extreme are the gnostics, who deny that Jesus came in human form. Acceptance of the work of the Holy Spirit for the cessationists and belief in the work on earth by Jesus in human form by the gnostics contradict each group's false concept of what they believe is holy versus what they believe is corrupt.

Cessationism and gnosticism are equally a denial of Jesus—one denies the current work of the Holy Spirit by selectively denying certain aspects of it that Scripture clearly does not deny, and the other denies the humanity of the Son of God and thereby strips Him of the very attributes Scripture attests He had when He walked the earth among us.

Thus, the cessationist critics of *The Harbinger*

who object to its prophetic role in warning America of impending judgment do so at their own peril, because this is the role and function of the Great Commission, part of which declares that the testimony of Jesus is the Spirit of prophecy. They are on the wrong side of prophetic history.

Chapter 15

DOES *THE HARBINGER* PREACH the GOSPEL?

T HE HARBINGER INDEED—AND very strongly—preaches the gospel of salvation. It includes an entire chapter on the reason and way of salvation, called "Eternity." Some have called this the most powerful presentation of salvation they've ever read. Is it thus very surprising (or perhaps not) that some critics have openly asserted that *The Harbinger* does not preach salvation or a call to repentance?

Yeshua—Jesus—Is Savior

The gospel message of repentance and salvation through the new birth offered to all through Jesus is woven throughout the pages of *The Harbinger*. In the chapter titled "Eternity," the gospel message is given in all its clarity and glory to the reader in a conversation between Nouriel Kaplan and the prophet.

The chapter begins with the prophet asking Nouriel Kaplan the question, "And what will you do on the Day of Judgment?"[1] A conversation between Nouriel and the prophet progresses from there. As the conversation continues, the prophet's questions become direct and personal. He asks Nouriel—and by extension also asks us:

> And what if it *were* you, Nouriel, living there at that time, walking in their sandals? What if it were you who heard the voice of the prophets, and understood the Harbingers, and knew the judgment was coming? Everyone around you was oblivious to it. Everyone just went on with their lives with no idea of what was coming. What would you do?"

Nouriel replies, "I'd want them to know, I'd want them to be saved. I'd tell them."

The prophet replies, "But who would listen to you? Who would take your warning seriously? And what about your own predicament? A nation's heading for judgment, but you're a part of it. How do you save yourself? What will *you* do on the Day of Judgment? Where will you go to find safety?"

Nouriel is clueless. He replies, "Outside the country, I guess."

But the prophet correctly points out to him:

> Judgment isn't a matter of geography. It doesn't matter where you are. No place is far enough away, and no refuge strong enough.

Nouriel understands what the prophet means and asks, "So what would I do?"

This allows the prophet to transition to the necessity of each person's personal accountability to God. He says:

The reason I ask is because you *do* live in such a time and place, and you *have* heard the voice of the prophets, and you *do* understand the Harbingers and know what they portend. So the question isn't hypothetical. And it's not even, "What *would* you do?" What *will* you do? What will you do, Nouriel, on the Day of Judgment?'

Nouriel still doesn't fully realize what the prophet means and asks, "On the day of a nation's judgment?"

But the prophet responds more directly:

On the day of *your* judgment....What if you were one of them, back then, and your life ended before the nation's judgment came? What then?[2]

In the course of their conversation, they discuss the need for judgment to do away with evil. The prophet says:

Because heaven would then be filled with locks and prisons, hatred, violence, fear, and destruction. Heaven would cease to be heaven...and would become hell instead. But there *is* a heaven, and there is a time and place of no more sorrow...no more hate...no more weeping or tears...and no more pain. There must be a judgment. Evil must end...beyond which is heaven.

Nouriel replies, "So, in other words, if evil entered heaven, heaven would cease to be heaven because it would have evil in it."[3]

As the conversation continues, they address man's fallen sinful nature and his evil inclination in the following manner:

"Yes," [the prophet] answered. "And who is evil?"

"Those who kill, who deceive, who steal, those who hurt and abuse others…"

"And that's it?" he asked.

"I'm sure there are other categories."

"And what about you, Nouriel? Do you fit into any of those categories?"

"No."

"No," he replied, "you wouldn't. But remember, *'All the ways of a man are right in his own eyes.'*[4] It's from the Book of Proverbs. That's human nature. So be careful of the image that appears in your own eyes. Beware of the good Nazi."

"The good Nazi? And what's that supposed to mean?"

"The Nazis sent millions to their deaths out of pure hatred and evil. Can you think of a people more evil than that? And yet do you think most of them saw themselves as evil?"

"No."

"And why not?" he asked. "Because they compared themselves and measured themselves by the standards they themselves created. Each, in his own eyes, was a good Nazi, a moral Nazi, a decent Nazi, a religious Nazi, and a Nazi no worse than the next. For by seeing themselves in their own eyes, they became blind. But their judgment would come in the form of destruction, and their sins would be exposed before the world."

"But there's a big difference between the Nazis and most people."

"The principle is the same. You can never judge yourself by your own standards and your own righteousness, but only in light of *His* [God's] righteousness."

"And how do we hold up in light of His righteousness?"

"Which do you think is greater," he asked, "the moral distance that separates us from the most monstrous of Nazis or that which separates us from God?"

"I guess that which separates us from God."

"That's correct, because the first separation is finite. But the second is infinite. So what we see as the slightest of sins within ourselves appears, in the eyes of Him who is absolute goodness, even more abhorrently evil than the crimes of the Nazis appear to us. In light of the absolute Good, our lust becomes as adultery and our hatred as murder."

"But then who could stand?" I asked. "Who could make it into heaven?"

"No one could stand, and no one could make it into heaven. How far would just one sin take you away from the infinite righteousness of God?"

"An infinite distance?"

"Yes. So how far are we from heaven?"

"An infinite distance."

"And how great is the judgment?"

"Infinitely great."

"And how long would it take to bridge the gap, to be reconciled to God, to enter heaven?"

"An infinity of time."

"Eternity," he said.

"So we could never get there, could we?"

"And to be infinitely separated from God and heaven...is what?" he asked.

"Hell?"

"Hell—infinite separation from God and from all things good; total, infinite, eternal judgment."[5]

This is just a sample, but it suffices for the
reader to see for himself that *The Harbinger* not
only presents the gospel, but it also presents an
enlightening discussion on the wages of sin, the
need for redemption, and how to obtain it from
the only source God has provided—Jesus the
Messiah.[6]

After reading *The Harbinger*, I have concluded
it is an egregious error of interpretation and mis-
judgment to assert it does not preach the gospel or
present the gospel in a manner that will compel
readers to search their own hearts to know their
own heart condition and response to the question,
"What will *you* do with Jesus?"

The question requires a depth of discernment
among God's people—real spiritual discernment—
because spiritual blindness to the message of salvation, wherever it is presented, including through
the message of *The Harbinger*, cannot be attrib-
uted to just willful ignorance. It is something
much deeper, much darker than that.

To be spiritually blind to the message of the
gospel, mischaracterizing the watchman, the servant of God, who presents that message, reveals
that we are dealing here with spiritual forces of
wickedness in high places, in the highest places
within the body of the Lord: within the realm of
those who believe they have been charged with
defending the Christian faith itself.

If, indeed, we have been spiritually infiltrated
at this level, as I believe we have, then the wickedness and deception is greater than we've realized,
and we need to truly discern the acts and behavior

of the people who are attempting to turn the body of Lord Jesus Christ against one another. The enemy has been permitted to use these distracters to squelch the call of God that is calling the people of this great nation to repent at this late hour in our nation's history.

Stumbling Blocks for Other Believers

The servants of God must be very careful in their assessment of the tools being used to share the gospel of Jesus with the lost. The means and methods are of little consequence, as long as the gospel is being shared. Paul writes:

> Who are you to judge the servant of another? To his own master he stands or falls; and he will stand, for the Lord is able to make him stand.
> —Romans 14:4

What matters is that the gospel is being preached, the nation is being called to repentance, and people are being led to Jesus and His salvation. Remember Paul's words: "For now we see in a mirror dimly...now I know in part" (1 Cor. 13:12). He included himself in this admonition, even though he was writing Scripture under the inspiration of the Holy Spirit. This indicates to the rest of us just how very careful we must be in these matters, and not become arrogant, thinking ourselves any higher than our peers in the faith, but living humbly in the grace of God and handling our differences in a quiet fashion and not making them public, lest we discredit our brothers, ourselves, and the faith we hold in God before an incredulous and fallen world.

Criticism for the Sake of Criticizing

Consider this. Would we find fault with the manner in which certain books of the Bible were written and how God was portrayed in them? For example, let's take the Book of Esther. No evangelical Christian or observant Jew would say this book is not inspired of the Lord and does not deserve a place in the Hebrew Bible.

Yet were we to use the same rigid and extremely narrow methods and criticisms employed by the critics of *The Harbinger*, the Book of Esther would have to be rewritten, or otherwise discarded from the canon, because God is not mentioned anywhere in it. And yet, lest we forget, *The Harbinger*, unlike most books—unlike even most Christian books—contains a full chapter presenting salvation!

Presenting the Gospel

One of the key aims of *The Harbinger* is the salvation of the lost. It not only presents ancient biblical mysteries, it not only sounds an alarm of warning and a wake-up call, and it not only constitutes a national call for repentance and revival, but it also presents salvation to all who need to be saved.

The chapter titled "Eternity," to which we have referred in this chapter, has one central purpose: to provide the reasons why salvation can only come through Jesus and to give the reader the reasons to believe and be saved.

Jonathan Cahn has said this about the message of his book:

> Whether it specifically includes such words as "you need to believe" or not, the entire chapter ["Eternity"] is telling the reader that they need to believe in Jesus. Similarly, it doesn't specifically state every title of Messiah (Son of God, Savior, the Lord, the Lamb), yet it does clearly identify Jesus as God Himself, generally considered to be a much more heavy, radical, and all embracing title. Further, it is stated that Jesus died for our sins and also overcame death, that His death was "to bear an infinite judgment, in which all sins are nullified and all who partake are set free…forgiven…saved. An infinite redemption in which judgment and death are overcome and a new life given…a new beginning…a new birth." As far as not including the fact that the Lord is coming again and that He will set up a millennial kingdom, while these are important statements of doctrine, they aren't requirements of leading someone to receive salvation.[7]

The Harbinger is not only the revelation of mysteries but also a trumpet call, an alarm, a wake-up call—a call for salvation, for revival, and for repentance to a nation badly in need of repenting. It is a trumpet call that is sounding across the land. Pastor Cahn poses this concluding thought:

> Believers in every camp hold to the very orthodox and biblical tenet that God does indeed judge

and does indeed warn of coming judgment. If so, we would have to be able to discern the signs of his warnings, just as we must discern the signs of the times. Most believers in America share the conviction that this nation is in rapid departure [from] God and His ways and in danger of judgment.

So then, the question must be asked:

If God were to send a warning of danger and judgment to America, what would such a warning sound like? Believers across America believe that it would sound identical to the message of *The Harbinger*. In fact, they believe it is sounding.

Let the reader read for himself. Let the hearer hear for himself. And let each believer seek and hearken to the voice and calling of God.[8]

Chapter 16

PROMOTING *THE HARBINGER* PROMOTES the GOSPEL

THE MESSAGE OF *The Harbinger*—a message of repentance, of seeking God, and of seeking His salvation in Jesus—is one that must get out by every means available and across every venue, because it is part of keeping the Great Commission to preach the gospel to all of creation. If the gospel is for everyone, any message that pertains to the gospel—like that of *The Harbinger*—ought to be heard and seen in every venue as well.

It is critically important for the message of the gospel to be released in the highways and byways of America, heralding a call to repentance and salvation, because we are living in a time when we are witnessing America turning its back on the godly foundation on which it was founded and on the plans and purposes of almighty God for this land.

And there are serious consequences for the nation that forgets God.

Washington's Prophetic Warning

The Harbinger reveals a prophetic warning, given to America on its first day as a fully formed nation in the first-ever presidential address. It was this:

> The propitious smiles of Heaven, can never be expected on a nation that disregards the eternal rules of order and right, which Heaven itself has ordained.[1]

What was President Washington saying here? He was saying this: America's blessings are based on its relationship with God. If America ever disregards or forgets or turns away from the eternal rules of order and right—the laws, the precepts, the standards, and the ways of God—if America ever departs from these, then the blessings of God will be withdrawn from the land.

Step by step, that's what America has done (and is doing). We have turned from God as a nation. We have removed Him from our lives. We have ruled Him out of our culture, out of our government, out of our economy, out of our public square, and out of the instruction and lives of our children. We have made God a stranger.

And as we have driven God from our national life, we have brought in other gods and idols to replace Him—gods of sensuality, materialism, violence, wealth, carnality, and sexual promiscuity. And as did Israel, so we too have abandoned the ways of God, the laws of God, and the standards of God, choosing immorality instead. The nation that was established to bring the Word and light of God to the world now fills the earth with pornography. We too now call evil "good," and good "evil." What we once knew to be immoral, we now celebrate, and what we once knew to be right, we now war against. American culture has turned in upon itself, a civilization at war against the very foundation on which it was established. And those who simply remain true to what was always known to be true are now vilified, marginalized, mocked, labeled "intolerant," increasingly banned from the public square, and ultimately persecuted.[2]

Promoting the Gospel or Apostasy?

As the message in *The Harbinger* is being read by millions of people and lives are being changed and challenged to repent and be saved, critics of the means and methods used to spread the gospel message have accused these evangelical Christians of apostasy from the faith for joining with other groups outside of the Christian evangelical sphere in the effort to bring America back to its godly foundations. These critics object to evangelical Christians combining efforts with other non-evangelical groups, such as those who are standing for biblical values and against America's moral descent. They charge these Christians with joining those who are fighting for the rights of America's unborn, whose lives are snuffed out before they even begin because of federally subsidized, taxpayer-funded abortion on demand. They object to evangelicals speaking out against a social, radical, humanistic agenda in our public school system and other trends that should alarm every Christian.

If an evangelical who is alarmed about what is

happening in our country wants to do something about organizing with other Americans against these trends, regardless of their personal profession of faith, is it possible that this person compromises his or her personal Christian faith in doing so, as some suggest?

If Moses were alive today, they would question what God had spoken to him about granting the Levites cities to live in with pastures for their cattle (Num. 35:1–8) because he had already said they had no inheritance in the land that Israel was about to possess (Num. 18:20; Deut. 10:9; 12:12; 14:27, 29; 18:1–2; Josh. 13:33).

Were Joshua living today, these people would rise up to criticize him for granting to the priests and Levites cities with their pasture lands (Josh. 21) that had been part of the inheritance apportioned to the other tribes when entering the Promised Land for the same reasons.

Criticism of the means and methods of spreading the gospel message has discounted the exceptions the Lord makes because of His grace and loving-kindness. They sacrifice the spirit of the Word—and with it, Christian orthopraxy[3]—at the altar of the letter of the Word.

Pharisees at Passover

This is like the classic pharisaical belief that to enter a Roman's home during the Passover, or at any time, would defile them and keep them from serving God. It is like the Pharisees who accused Jesus of breaking the Law because He and His disciples picked heads of grain in order to eat on the Sabbath. Our Lord rebuked them by reminding them that David did the same when he and his men "entered the house of God, and they ate the consecrated bread, which was not lawful for him to eat nor for those with him, but for the priests alone" (Matt. 12:4; see also 1 Sam. 21:1–6; Matt. 12:1–7; Mark 2:23–28; Luke 6:1–5).

It has always been this way. We see the same dynamics in the Gospels, where Jesus is criticized by the religious leaders of His day for socializing with what they considered the dregs of society (Matt. 9:10–13; Mark 2:15–17; Luke 5:27–32).

Believers today should be encouraged to use discernment in aligning with social or cultural groups in order to spread the gospel message, but they should never be discouraged from finding creative, practical ways to tell others of the hope and salvation that can be found in God. The message of *The Harbinger* calls us to be "watchmen on the gate," warning others of the peril of turning away from God and of the reward and blessing of God that come to those who call upon His name. The apostle Paul expressed it this way: "I have become all things to all men, so that I may by all means save some" (1 Cor. 9:22).

The Call to Repentance

The Great Commission of our Lord begins with His command to all His followers in Matthew's Gospel: "Go therefore and make disciples of all the nations, baptizing them in the name of the Father and the Son and the Holy Spirit, teaching them to observe all that I commanded you; and lo,

I am with you always, even to the end of the age" (Matt. 28:19–20).

In Mark's Gospel, the Great Commission to preach the gospel to "all the nations" is expanded to include "all creation." It is obvious that the Lord Jesus wanted all of His disciples to fully grasp what He meant the first time around, so this time He included "all creation" in order to emphasize its importance to everyone listening within earshot:

> And He said to them, "Go into all the world and preach the gospel to all creation. He who has believed and has been baptized shall be saved; but he who has disbelieved shall be condemned."
> —MARK 16:15–16

There was to be no exception as to where they were to go, who they were to share this good news with, to whom they would be addressing themselves, or the distance, nation, race, ethnic group, or religious order, because it included the injunction to preach this message throughout the entire habitable world—all of creation.

The Harbinger's message—a call of repentance and of turning to God and His salvation in Jesus— is one that includes all people, regardless of the limitations above, because it is based upon the foundation of Jesus and a call to accept His salvation through repentance and faith in Him. When Jesus gave His disciples and all who would follow afterward His Great Commission, He did not set parameters as to where they were or were not to go and to whom they were or were not to speak.

His injunction to all of us who call ourselves followers of Jesus was that we preach the gospel—His good news—to everyone without exception, and that we'd go to the ends of the earth doing so.

I am convinced by the evidence that can be seen that the Lord is speaking to this nation through the message contained in *The Harbinger*. Who are we—or anyone, for that matter—to criticize and lay restrictions on whom we may share or not share this message with?

Pastor Cahn has gone into all the world to preach the gospel, and the gospel of Israel and the world's hope is needed here in America right now more than ever before, because our society—our entire nation—has been overrun by secular humanistic progressives and Marxist intellectuals.

What Others Have Said About the Salvation Message of *The Harbinger*

Two prominent, well-respected pastors wrote open letters to those attacking *The Harbinger*. In doing so, they both specifically addressed the book's call to salvation. Allow me to share what each of these men wrote:

> And for [a critic]...to say that the Gospel is not clearly presented is pure fabrication. You can't find a clearer presentation than what it given in chapter 21 than Jonathan gives; how to get saved, how to be born again, that Jesus is the Jewish Messiah; and many people who are not believers are having the opportunity of reading a novel that is not fictional, but factual, even though written in novel form. I believe many

people's eternal destinies are being changed by
Jonathan's insights into the similarities between
ancient Israel and what has happened in our
country over the last decade.[4]

—DWIGHT DOUVILLE

This is puzzling and quite disturbing to me, especially when Mr. Cahn is implied by some (not all)
of his critics of the condemning sort to not have
Jesus Christ or the gospel message of salvation
anywhere in the book. Chapter twenty-one of
The Harbinger has one of the strongest, Christ-
centered salvation messages to be found in fiction or in nonfiction, if anyone cares to check
the facts. What is most distressing is that those
critics…would write such things, knowing they
aren't telling the truth.[5]

—TERRY JAMES

The Strategies of Hell

It must be asked: If the devil would look upon
American evangelicals, perhaps the largest Christian group in the United States today, and strate-
gize to bench them from becoming active, what do
you think he would do? I'll tell you. It's very easy
and very simple. He would:

1. Have them disagree over whether or
   not Christians can and should join
   with others in the national debates on
   the issues and topics that most concern Americans in general and Jews and
   Christians in particular.

2. Have them fight amongst themselves by creating one or more watchdog groups against another group or groups with whom they disagree.

3. Have them write books and articles focusing primarily against other Christians to warn them of the others' apostasy, even calling out longtime mainline Christian leaders, pastors, and evangelists whom they accuse of apostasy, compromise, and even heresy in some extreme cases.

4. Turn them into spiritual neurotics and introverts who turn in on themselves rather than evangelize and become forces for real revival across this land.

5. Introduce destructive heresies, such as cessationism or replacement theology on one side and extreme Pentecostalism (spiritual emotionalism without discernment of spirits) on the other, as well as other false doctrines.

Armchair Bloggers and Friendly Fire

I would caution my brethren—be they Jewish or Christian—that one need not compromise one's faith to stand for truth. Those who stand with others with whom they may have a disagreement with concerning matters of faith to fight against the immoral and corrupt forces arrayed against our nation at this hour are not compromising

their core beliefs but are practicing precisely what
Jesus and His brother James enjoined all Christians and Jews to do: be the salt of the earth (Matt.
5:13); a light unto the world (v. 14); and doers of
the Word, not just hearers who delude themselves
(James 1:22).

Our nation already has too many "armchair
bloggers" quick to criticize others who are making a real difference in their service to God and to
our nation. All these people have done is create a
generation of critics to hound those who are doing
something about the ills these people so often
complain about.

If Americans of moral character, regardless
of personal religious conviction, do not stand
together—there is strength in numbers—to com-
bat the rising moral decay and corruption in our
government, our civil institutions, and our popular culture, they will be held accountable as watchmen who did not sound the alarm when danger
approached (Ezek. 33:1–9). *The Harbinger* is
sounding the alarm, and already more than a million people have heeded its warning, as attested
to by its sale of over one million copies across
this nation and its continual status of being on
the *New York Times* best-seller list since it first
appeared in paperback.

America became great because the blessings of
almighty God shone on its land and because its
people, by and large, honored God, revered His
Word, and kept His commandments even within
civil law. They honored God and worshipped Him

and would not compromise their faith in public office or the workplace. How much has changed!

America arose because of the bedrock of its Judeo-Christian foundation—this even in spite of the activities and beliefs of some of its founders. If the day comes when America passes into history as just another great civilization that saw its rise only to fall within three centuries, it will not be because God had anything to do with it but because its people forsook the Lord their God. It will be because when He sounded the alarm through some of His people, as *The Harbinger* does, some sat idly by while others sought to oppose those sounding the warning.

But if America is to see redemption, it will be because of those who heard the warnings and took heed. As we witness America's free fall into moral and spiritual apostasy, it is not a time for parlor discussions. Rather, it is the time for watchmen. And the watchmen must stand guard on the walls, disregarding both applause and jeers, and blow as loudly and strongly as they can, so those who would hear the sound will be saved.

Chapter 17

The FALL of SAM

THE LAST SEVERAL chapters have explained to you the truth about *The Harbinger* and have cleared up the misunderstandings some people have had. With that same goal in mind I have written this next-to-last chapter as a story, an illustration. In the same way Jesus used parables to teach His followers important truths, I believe the story in this chapter employs that type of approach and will be helpful to you, the reader, in clarifying the accusations, confusions, and the real truth concerning *The Harbinger*.

Imagine with me a man named Sam who grew up loving the Lord. He serves in his church. He leads Bible studies. He's had some challenges and rough times, but all in all, he's considered himself a very blessed man.

He's always identified with King David as a man after God's heart. The Lord has always spoken to his heart through the life of King David and the psalms. But something has happened to Sam. He's grown cold in his walk with God. And he's been increasingly tempted by his secretary. The two have flirted with each other. They've shared lunched together. Sam's marriage has become strained. Nothing physical has taken

186

place with his secretary, but it's on the verge of becoming adultery. Sam is entertaining thoughts of having a relationship, even if it means leaving his wife and family.

Sam has loved and served the Lord for years, but now he's in danger of destroying his faith, his marriage, his family, his Christian witness, and his life. Although the Bible promises that God will lead and shepherd His children, Sam isn't listening to the leading of the Spirit or his conscience. So the Lord begins to intervene to wake him up.

The Signs of Warning

Sam turns on the radio in his bedroom. It's a secular station, but it is Sunday, so a sermon about King David's temptation to commit adultery is on the air. The next week Sam gets in his car and turns on the radio to a different station, another secular one. But it's Sunday again, and the station happens to be playing a sermon. The preacher is speaking about David's fall in adultery.

A couple of days later he turns on the television to a talk show. The theme for that episode is adultery. Then on a trip to the library, a book falls off of the shelf, a children's book on the life of David.

In the middle of that week Sam decides to stop by a local church to sit in on their Bible study. The Bible study leader is teaching on the prophet Nathan's confrontation of David over his hidden sin.

Sam then has a dream of unusual clarity. He sees two bearded men in football jerseys. On the front of one man's shirt is the number eleven. On the front of the other one's shirt is the number two. On the back of their shirts is the name *Sam*. Sam doesn't know what it means, but the dream haunts him. Everything is haunting him.

The Message of the Warning

Sam goes to a Christian friend and tells him about these occurrences but holds back from telling him about his temptation. The friend tells him that all these occurrences are consistent. God is trying to get through to him.

The friend asks him if he is in danger of committing adultery. Sam breaks down and confesses what's been happening in his life. He then tells his friend of the dream. The friend immediately begins interpreting it. There are two men named Sam. "Second Samuel" he says. "And what were the numbers again?" he asks.

"One man's shirt had an eleven on it, and the other was a two," replies Sam.

"Let's open to 2 Samuel, chapter 11, verse 2." So they do. And this is the verse they find:

> Now when evening came David arose from his bed and walked around on the roof of the king's house, and from the roof he saw a woman bathing; and the woman was very beautiful in appearance.

The friend tells Sam, "God is calling to you. He's warning you, Sam. God is merciful. He loves you. So of course He's going to warn you. He doesn't want you to fall. He's using His Word to speak to you. And you've always identified with

David, so the Lord is speaking to you through David's life.

"You're in danger. You're at risk of destroying everything in your life that means something. God is speaking to you. You have to take it very seriously. Cut off the relationship immediately, before it's too late. Repent of this, Sam, and turn back to God. His arms are open."

The Counsel of Thirteen

But Sam wants a second opinion. He knows of a group of men who gather in a Bible study nearby, thirteen men who profess to be discerning judges of sound and false doctrine. He goes to their study. While not divulging his personal situation concerning his secretary, he tells the men present of the strange events taking place in his life and the warning that his friend gave him. One by one the men in the group each begin an attempt to shoot down the warning given to him.

1. The hermeneutic accusation

The first man from the group attacks the warning by telling Sam, "Your friend is using bad hermeneutics and is misapplying the Word of God. He's ripping scriptures out of their context and giving a false interpretation. Second Samuel is about King David. It takes place three thousand years ago. You can't apply that to you. The proper interpretation is that it's about David's situation not yours."

Sam and King David: Of course Sam's friend has done nothing of the kind. He's never once suggested that 2 Samuel is about anyone but King David. Rather, he is saying that circumstances in Sam's life are similar to King David's situation and God is simply using the scriptures concerning David to speak to and warn Sam of his predicament and future.

To apply a scripture to a circumstance other than its original circumstance is in no way "ripping it out of context." In fact, as we have seen, Scripture itself does this very thing. Further, to apply the "ripping charge" to the simple observance or revelation that God is using His Scriptures to speak to a person or nation is even more absurd.

America and Ancient Israel: So too the accusation that *The Harbinger* is in any way touching the hermeneutics of Isaiah 9:10 is absurd. It fully affirms that it is a prophetic word to Israel but that God is simply using the scriptures concerning Israel before its fall to speak to another nation in a similar circumstance: America.

2. The "You're not in covenant" accusation

A second man from the group attacks the warning by telling Sam, "Your friend is in error. He's telling you that you have a special covenant with God. King David had a special covenant with God. God was correcting David as a man who had a special covenant with Him. You don't have a special covenant with God. Therefore none of the things that applied to David's situation and God's dealing with it can apply to you."

Sam and King David: Again, the charge has

nothing to do with the friend's counsel. Nothing the friend told Sam requires that Sam had a covenant with God as King David did. His friend's counsel was simply that he, like David, knew God and that he, also like David, was in danger of falling into adultery.

America and Ancient Israel: So too the covenant accusation thrown at *The Harbinger* equally holds no weight. Nothing that *The Harbinger* says concerning America requires that America has a special covenant with God, but it simply says that America is in danger of falling, as was Israel.

3. The "It's not significant" accusation

A third man from the group attacks the warning by telling Sam, "Even though what's happened in your life looks significant, there's really no significance to it. Haven't there been other times in your life when you heard a scripture about David? And weren't there other times in your life when you heard other scriptures or pastors give a message that touched your heart or life? So you see, it really doesn't mean anything."

"What about the fact that three different ministers were all speaking about the exact same thing?" asked Sam.

"Ministers have to speak about some account in the Bible," responds the man, "so why not the account of David? Everybody knows David. David is famous and loved. And his fall is a good example of warning. And we live in a day when sexual sin is prevalent, so of course they spoke about that. I'm sure there are many pastors speaking about

David in any given week. There's nothing significant about it."

"What about the book on David that happened to fall out of the shelf?" Sam asks.

"Someone either didn't put the book back right or moved it off center. Gravity did the rest. Books fall. So what? There had to be other times in your life when a book fell off a bookshelf and it didn't mean anything. And there's very little consistency in these things. You said that one pastor was speaking of David's temptation. Another was speaking about a different event, Nathan's rebuke. And the book that fell was simply about David, not specifically about his fall. Don't listen to your friend. He's just manipulating things, putting on a magic show of illusions, just to scare you."

Sam and King David: The attempt to debunk the significance of the signs is extremely misleading. Whether or not the man heard and was touched by other scriptures about David during his lifetime or whether he had been touched by other scriptures has no relevance. The relevant point is, the specific scripture or case came up again and again within a short span of time. There are countless scriptures that can be on television and radio, not to mention all the non-Christian content that is on secular media. In short, it is extremely statistically significant.

Similarly, their argument about other pastors speaking of David is also misleading. There are thousands upon thousands of pastors in America. But for one man to hear the same thing, again and again, out of a pool of just a few pastors or messages is, again, extremely statistically significant. Further, it is the consistency shared by these events that is the significant factor, not the differences.

As for the explanation on the falling book, this is irrelevant. Sam's friend never suggested that the book fell supernaturally or by the hand of an angel, but rather that it fell by natural means. That wasn't the point. The point was that in this context, it was another sign linked to David—and again another extremely statistically significant event. Add to this the fact that it is not one or two events, but several—and the significance becomes multiplied and compounded.

America and Ancient Israel: So too the attempt to downplay the significance of the harbingers and events revealed in *The Harbinger* is extremely misleading. To try to argue them away by saying that they were natural occurrences is irrelevant as, again, no one has argued that the events were caused by direct supernatural intervention such as the hands of angels. The fact that events in this world have natural causation does not in the slightest way take away from any significance, just as the fact that Messiah was crucified by natural means, by human courts and trials, human soldiers, nails of metal, and an execution stake of wood in no way takes away the prophetic significance of the event.

And the attempt to brush off the fact that *every one* of the signs of judgment were manifested, and each prominently manifested in connection to the same event, 9/11, and each consistent with the other, compounding the phenomenon—as if it weren't significant—is mind-bogglingly misleading. On top of that, all these are capped off by the actual proclamation of the actual specific verse of Isaiah 9:10, also linked to 9/11—and from the most prominent of American leaders—making the attempts to dismiss these things hopeless.

And this is not even to touch on such inconvenient facts such as the greatest crash in American history happened to happen on the exact biblical day that happens to be connected to the wiping away of financial accounts, down to the date and hours—not only the greatest crash, but the two greatest crashes in American history up to those dates. Again, the enterprise is hopeless.

4. The "You've had worse" accusation

A fourth man attacks the warning by telling Sam, "You've had times in your life when you've gone through difficulties?"

"Yes," answers Sam.

"Like what?" the man asks.

"I've had tragedies. My child was injured in an accident and in the hospital for months. We've almost gone bankrupt."

"And have you made any major mistakes or had some major sins in your life?"

"Yes," admits Sam.

"So then," says the man, "why didn't God speak to you then, when you needed it more? Or why didn't you take those other events in your life as God speaking to you? I don't know what you're going through now, but if He didn't speak to you then, you shouldn't take these things as His speaking to you now."

Sam and King David: The issue here is not whether there have been other crises in Sam's life. The issue is simply whether God is calling him. The fact is that Sam is morally and spiritually in greater danger than he's ever been in his life, but that is not necessarily evident to those around him.

America and Ancient Israel: So too the argument that America has had other calamities and with more people being killed doesn't hold. God's warnings and callings are never dependent on how one tragedy compares to another. Warnings and judgments can involve one person, millions, or about three thousand as in the judgment of those who rebelled at Mt. Sinai. Beyond that America has never been in greater moral and spiritual danger than it is right now. That would argue all the more for the need of God's warning and calling.

5. The "So you're saying it's speaking about you" accusation

A fifth man attacks the warning by telling Sam, "This is all ridiculous. Your friend is giving you false doctrine. He's telling you that 2 Samuel is speaking about you. So that's what you think? You think the scriptures in 2 Samuel are really about you and not David? Or he's telling you that the scripture was written about both David *and* you? That you are the fulfillment of those scriptures? That they were prophesying of your situation? That's ridiculous!"

Sam and King David: Indeed it would be

ridiculous if Sam's friend had said anything of the
kind, but he didn't. He said rather that God was
using the scriptures concerning King David's fall
to speak to Sam about his life. In no way is that
comparable to saying that the scriptures concerning King David were really about Sam.

America and Ancient Israel: Ridiculous too—
not to mention confused—is the accusation made
by some critics that *The Harbinger* claims Isaiah
9:10 was prophesying of America or that it was
speaking of America in addition to ancient Israel.
To say that a scripture and scriptural example is
being used to speak to a modern nation is light-
years removed from claiming that the scripture is
actually prophesying of the modern nation. This
is a basic foundational confusion and colossal flaw
in most of the attacks made on *The Harbinger*. *The
Harbinger* says no such thing, and this attack has
not become any less wrong or ridiculous with age.

6. The "You're replacing David" accusation

A sixth man attacks the warning by telling
Sam, "So, you mean to tell me that your friend
told you that you were replacing David? You, Sam,
are the new David? That God's promises to David
and his line are no longer in effect, but now He's
chosen you as David's replacement? You're not
King David! You might have identified with him.
But I'm sorry, your friend is giving you false doctrine. You're not King David!"

Sam and King David: Sam's friend never told
him that he has replaced David. He has only said
that God has used the example and scriptures

concerning King David to speak to him, and that this makes sense in view of Sam's long identification with Israel's ancient king. The attack is beyond foolish.

America and Ancient Israel: So too the accusation against *The Harbinger* on the grounds of replacement theology is beyond foolish. *The Harbinger* never advocates any form of replacement theology in any way. Replacement theology claims that God has replaced Israel with the church. This has no place in *The Harbinger* (without even dealing with the fact that Jonathan Cahn is Jewish!).

Even the replacement theology argument itself had to be altered to say that *The Harbinger* claimed Israel was replaced *by America*. This was based on the fact that *The Harbinger* mentions that America's first founders, the Puritans, saw America as a new Israel. As noted earlier, the statement isn't a theological one; it's pure history. If one takes offense at historical fact, there's little that can be done, but that's the fact. It is brought up only to show America's identification with ancient Israel and that it would logically follow that God could speak to such a nation through the example of ancient Israel, especially when America now finds itself following the pattern of that nation's apostasy and fall.

7. The "It's not exactly exact" accusation

A seventh man attacks the warning by telling Sam, "Your friend is misleading you. He's twisting the facts. He's trying to connect you to what's in the Bible, but he's manipulating things. It doesn't match. David was the king of Israel? Are you a king? No, you're an accountant. It doesn't match. David lived in a palace. You live in a regular house. David had more than one wife. You just have one. It doesn't connect. David was walking on his rooftop when he saw a woman bathing. Now, I don't know what you're dealing with, but have you walked on your rooftop lately? Your roof isn't even flat as was David's roof, another difference. You don't have neighbors who are bathing outside, do you? You see, your friend tried to make you think that it was the same. But on close inspection, you can see that these are two totally different situations. It has nothing to do with you. Don't lose sleep over it."

Sam and King David: The problem is Sam's friend never said he was a king or that everything in King David's situation had to be exactly the same as everything in the life of Sam. It's a ridiculous proposition as everything couldn't be the same or it would be the same situation.

Further, the attack rests on the idea that Sam's friend was telling him that his situation was the fulfillment of a scriptural prophecy, in which case it would have to match whatever was spoken. But this misses the point and has nothing to do with the situation. Sam's friend is telling him that God is *speaking* to him through these signs and events, not *fulfilling* the scripture in his life. It would, again, follow that such absurd logic would require Jesus, as the Lamb of God, to have wool and be the exact match to the sacrificial lambs in the Book of Leviticus.

America and Ancient Israel: So also with *The Harbinger* some have sought to find any differences they could, any different details between the modern harbingers in America and that in the ancient case of Israel in order to argue away the significance of the phenomena. So they come with such arguments as, "The buildings in New York City weren't made of clay bricks," "The terrorists weren't exactly the same as the ancient Assyrians," or "The sycamore that was struck down in America was the American sycamore, while the sycamore that was struck down in ancient Israel was the Israeli sycamore," and so on—as if any of these things in any way disproved the phenomena or as if *The Harbinger* was saying that Isaiah 9:10 was prophesying of America. It was and is irrelevant on both counts. The harbingers, the signs of national judgment, are exactly that: signs of judgment, not fulfillments of prophecy.

As noted earlier, if every detail was to be exactly the same as every detail in ancient Israel, we wouldn't be dealing with America but with ancient Israel alone—only the same circumstance can produce the exact same details. And as noted before, according to such logic, the only way such people could be reached by *The Harbinger* is if 9/11 involved ancient Assyrians hurling spears at modern skyscrapers built entirely of clay bricks. Of course, ancient Assyrians wouldn't exist on 9/11, but such logic leads to such absurdities.

The overwhelming reality of what *The Harbinger* reveals—the amazing progression, the precise manifestations, the striking consistency of the totality—is what is involved. In other words, if God were to warn America of judgment using a biblical template, this is exactly what we would expect. And the fact that American leaders used the *exact same words of the exact same ancient vow* to respond to the calamity—the critics can only resort to other means ("They didn't really mean it," etc.) to attempt to explain it. The honest reaction even by a cautious observer is, "There does certainly seem to be something major going on."

8. The "God doesn't speak anymore" accusation

An eighth man attacks the warning by telling Sam, "God doesn't do things like this anymore. The Bible was finished in the first century, and God does not speak to His children apart from their reading His Word. How can you say that God is warning you? How do you know? And if God does speak to you or show you something, that would have to be 'extra-biblical revelation.' And since God is finished revealing, the idea that He would be trying to speak to you through these things is heresy."

Sam and King David: The problem is nothing in the Bible says that God doesn't "do things like this anymore." This would be a cessationist argument. There are certainly people who reside at one extreme of the spectrum where they regularly seek signs of God in cloud formations. But what is proposed here is another extreme. It goes beyond even hyper-cessationism to say that God is, in effect, entirely mute beyond what someone reads written in His Word. This doesn't line up with the most basic scriptures that speak of God leading His children, guiding them, and shepherding them. If God cannot speak in any way to His people, how can He lead them, guide them, and shepherd them through every circumstance of their lives?

Or perhaps what is imagined is a God who cannot speak through circumstance. But such a God would be entirely unbiblical. According to this view, a believer could never really know what God is saying, nor would one know where God is guiding him. According to this view, God could never correct His children. For how can one be corrected by God if one can never know what God is saying or doing? But the Bible clearly says that God does correct His children. Similarly, according to this view, God could never send warning. This has to be rejected as the Bible makes clear that God indeed does send warning. Thus this extreme view and limiting of God has to be rejected.

America and Ancient Israel: So with *The Harbinger* some critics have argued that God cannot speak in this way or that we can never know what God is ever saying through circumstance—which is, in effect, saying that God is mute. Even the most classic and conservative of Bible commentaries declares this to be entirely unbiblical. God clearly warns of judgment. If we cannot ever know that God is warning, then God could never warn and the Bible would be contradicted.

God does, indeed, use circumstances to communicate. And in the case of the harbingers, this communication is specific, precise, and consistent, and it is given clear meaning because they join together to a specific scripture of national judgment.

9. The mysticism accusation

A ninth man attacks the warning by telling Sam, "Your friend is advocating mysticism. Can God really talk through a children's book and through its falling off a shelf? Does every book that falls off a shelf mean it's a message from God? God speaking through the radio, through a dream, through a children's book—it's too mystical. And I heard that your friend believes the kabbalah, since he quoted from it in a teaching. God is not warning you of anything."

Sam and King David: This has more to do with the ninth man's very narrow and limiting view of God than anything else. The Bible gives example after example of God speaking through all things—from prophets to circumstances to signs to nature to historical events, etc. This very narrow view of God would label any such thing as "mystical," as if the words *mystical* or *mystery* were bad or unbiblical concepts.

This argument is built on a misconception. The ancient mystery religions used the word *mystery* to refer to things that were to be kept hidden. But the apostle Paul used the word *mystery* to refer to things that were hidden but that were now revealed. The God of Scripture is a God who reveals that which is hidden.

To say that there are no more things to be revealed is akin to claiming that one possesses all knowledge. But this would mean that there is no more insight, that there are no more things to be discovered in Scripture, that there is nothing more to be revealed about God's Word, and no more of God's leading of His people through life. But as long as there are things to be known and taught that one does not at first know, then those things remain mysteries until being revealed.

America and Ancient Israel: The Harbinger uses the word *mystery* in the same sense that Paul used it, as something that is not yet known to the reader and is yet to be revealed. If one believes that one knows all things, then one might as well stop reading any books or listening to any sermons.

As long as God is God and infinite, and man is man and finite, there will be mysteries on our side of the equation. As to God revealing His will or speaking through circumstance and events, this is hardly mystical, but is part of His everyday workings as revealed in Scripture.

10. The "That makes him a prophet" accusation

A tenth man attacks the warning by telling Sam, "If your friend is telling you that God is calling you, then your friend is speaking for God. Therefore, your friend is telling you God said something that is apart from the Bible, and your friend must be claiming to be a prophet. Since we don't believe there are prophets anymore, he must be a false prophet. Or even if we did believe that there could be prophets, he can't be a prophet because as my other friends told you earlier, he's twisting the Word. So he's a false prophet. Don't listen to his warning."

Sam and King David: The problem with this argument goes beyond the issue of whether one believes that people can now be called prophets or not. It claims, in effect, that if you say things such as, "God led me in this direction," "The Lord put on my heart that....," or "God really woke me up," then technically, you're speaking for God, and you're saying God said things that are not recorded in the Bible. Therefore, you're a prophet. This is an extreme view of God and Scripture. The friend of Sam is not even using words such as, "God put this on my heart," but is simply identifying a precise pattern of events as a warning to Sam. To take this and argue that this is a claim to prophethood is ludicrous. It would end up, in effect, making most believers prophets and most of these, false prophets.

America and Ancient Israel: *The Harbinger* identifies a precise pattern of events linked to a biblical progression and template. This progression and template is clearly one of judgment. To somehow get from this that this is a claim of prophethood is ludicrous. Most end-time prophecy books are filled with observers stating what God is doing or what current events mean, but nobody charges that these are equivalent to claims of prophethood. Beyond that, when the critics of *The Harbinger* tell their listeners or readers that these things are not warnings from God, and that God is not, in this way, warning America of judgment, how are they not doing the very thing they accuse others of doing? How are they not speaking for God?

11. The "Bible doesn't say to use it" accusation

An eleventh man attacks the warning by telling Sam, "There's nothing in the Bible that says that the situation of David is a pattern that can be applied to others or used by God to speak. Therefore you have to reject the warning your friend gave you."

Sam and King David: The problem with this is the Bible doesn't have to say that the example of David is a pattern that can be used. God can use any biblical example, any biblical passage, any biblical person to speak and communicate. Beyond that the New Testament clearly states that "these things"—those things written in the Old Testament—"were written for our instruction" (1 Cor. 10:11).

America and Ancient Israel: To say as one critic has claimed that one can't use the example of ancient Israel as a pattern is to exceed the bounds of Scripture. Since Scripture already says that these things are written for our instruction, how do such critics get the authority to say what can be used and what cannot? And from where do they derive the authority to say what God can use and what He can't? Certainly not from Scripture.

12. The "He's claiming to reveal the hidden meaning of an ancient scripture" accusation

A twelfth man attacks the warning by telling Sam, "Your friend is claiming that he knows the hidden meaning of the ancient scriptures about David. He's saying that no one knew the meaning of this scripture until he did. He's claiming to have discovered the hidden interpretation that no one else up to this time has known. You can't listen to anyone claiming such things."

Sam and King David: The problem with this is that Sam's friend is neither claiming nor doing any such thing. He is in no way claiming that there is a long hidden meaning to the scriptures about David that is only now in modern times being revealed. Rather, what's involved here is entirely different. What is new is not the revealing of a scripture's real and hidden meaning. Rather, what is new is what is happening in Sam's life, the unfolding events. Sam's friend is just helping him to see the clear message in it. That message happens to be a scriptural one that employs the case of King David.

Saying that God can speak to us through His Scriptures and use events in our lives to do it is in no way equivalent to saying that this is the revealing of a hidden meaning in ancient Scriptures that has been dormant for thousands of years. In fact, Sam's friend has not revealed or claimed to reveal anything new about the meaning of the Scriptures concerning David, only that there is a clear pattern in the recent events of Sam's life that link up with the case and example of King David.

America and Ancient Israel: In the case of *The Harbinger* critics have made the same charge and the same glaringly confused mistake. *The Harbinger* never claims to be revealing the true meaning of Isaiah 9:10 after thousands of years. Nor does it even claim to give new insight into what it means. What it does do is entirely different.

It gives revelation concerning a series of modern events that link up with the biblical template of the judgment of ancient Israel as concerning a scripture in Isaiah. This does not in the slightest way change, modify, alter, or even touch the original meaning of Isaiah 9:10.

13. The "Call to salvation" accusation

And lastly, the thirteenth man attacks the warning by telling Sam, "When your friend told you to turn to God, did he mention the name of Jesus? Did he tell you that you have to confess your sins and ask forgiveness by the blood of Jesus? Did he even tell you which God to turn to? It could have been another god. He didn't tell you anything that would lead you to redemption or to the true God. All the more reason to reject the warning he gave you."

Sam and King David: The problem with this charge is that what Sam's friend told him was entirely sufficient for the situation. There could be no question in Sam's mind that his friend was only referring to the God of the Bible and finding mercy in God through the blood of Jesus. To need explaining beyond this would give nitpicking new meaning.

The fact that the thirteenth man is spending his time attacking the very needed call of repentance given by Sam's friend, instead of actually seeking to help him find God's will in his life, as his friend did, speaks volumes. In all the conversations of the thirteen men with Sam, not one of them has sought to guide him toward repentance or the mercy and will of God. That was only done by Sam's friend.

America and Ancient Israel: In the same way, the call to salvation in *The Harbinger* is entirely sufficient for its purpose—to be the process of leading someone to salvation. There are few, if any, readers, who would not know that it's speaking of the Jesus who died on the cross and rose from death. The death of Jesus is, in fact, described in good detail, and the overcoming of death is clearly referring to the resurrection.

But beyond this, the fact that such critics of *The Harbinger* choose to spend their time attacking the call to salvation of others, while not spending any noticeable amount of time actually leading others to salvation as Jonathan Cahn has done, has been viewed by many as disgraceful. The fact that *The Harbinger*, unlike most books, secular or Christian, contains an entire chapter aimed at leading the reader to God should have been celebrated by these critics instead of condemned. The fact that it wasn't speaks volumes of those doing the criticizing and nothing concerning *The Harbinger*.

The Fall of Sam

So Sam has been told by the men not to listen to his friend's warning and that the signs of warning don't really mean anything. He agrees. He ends up not heeding the warning. He ends up falling into adultery. His marriage is destroyed, his family, his witness, his life—all destroyed because he didn't heed the warning given to him by God.

In the same way, some of the critics described throughout this book have seen it as their mission to attack the warning of *The Harbinger*. Many began doing so without even reading the book. What motivates such people to try to convince those who would be warned, not to be warned, remains a mystery. But the stakes involved in such a situation and the responsibility of those involved are as high as they could possibly be. To illustrate this, I give you one more analogy.

A House on Fire

It's morning. There's smoke coming out of a house in a suburban neighborhood. There's a family inside. But they're all sleeping. One of their neighbors, a local firefighter, is walking by when he notices something is wrong. He sees the smoke; he assesses its nature and location. He immediately realizes that the situation is extremely dangerous and the house can go up in flames at any time.

He shouts up at the house toward the bedroom, but they remain asleep. He rushes to the front door, but it's locked. He starts seeking to pry it open. He stops for a moment, gets on his cell phone, and calls for help.

In the process of all these attempts to help, other neighbors have gathered around him. They take issue with what he's trying to do. One says to those gathered, "Do we really know there's a fire? I know it may look like another fire we had a number of years ago that began the same way, but there are many differences. That fire took place in an old house and the construction materials were highly flammable. You can't apply the case of the old house to that of the new house. The firefighter is an alarmist. He's not applying things correctly. He's trying to make others afraid. How does he know the house is on fire? There can be smoke without fire. The smoke could be coming from an oven or a broken fireplace, who knows. But what he's doing is causing a disturbance. And that's not good for the neighborhood."

So the neighbors make it their aim to do everything they can to convince everyone around them that there's really no fire and not to listen to any alarm or any disturbance the firefighter may cause. They argue with the firefighter as he tries to get into the house. They claim he's causing damage and should stop what he's doing.

Then the neighbors realize that the firefighter has called the fire department to tell them to come down. So the neighbors also put in a call to the fire department and argue that it's all a false alarm. They continue making their arguments that the smoke doesn't necessarily mean a fire and that there are differences between what's happening at this house and the former fire. They do this all as the firefighter frantically tries to save the family. One of the neighbors quickly prints out their arguments against the idea that there's a real fire to be alarmed about and then begins to circulate the papers throughout the neighborhood.

When the fire truck arrives, they gather around the firefighters to convince them that the fire isn't real. They also want to know how fast the fire truck was going as it rushed to the house, and did they go over the speed limit or not.

Meanwhile, the family is asleep inside the house in danger of destruction. *Will they be saved?*

When all is said and done, that remains the question.

Chapter 18

WHAT'S NEXT?

T HE HARBINGER IS a critical and timely wake-
up call to a nation that desperately needs it.
It is a lifeguard sending help to a drowning man,
even though that man is fighting the lifeguard
tooth and nail—a typical survival instinct and
human reaction brought on by raw fear and panic,
the same kind of fear and panic Adam and Eve
experienced as they heard God approach after
their fall.

The message of *The Harbinger* is much more
than a supernatural thriller. It is a bone-chilling
account of the refusal of America to heed God's
warnings of judgment. It is an almost-too-
amazing-to-be-true revelation of how the same
prophetic warnings of national judgment that
appeared in the last days of ancient Israel have
now reappeared on American soil in stunning
and eerie precision.

Jonathan Cahn believes that 2012, the year
The Harbinger first appeared, was a tipping point
for our nation. He points out that 2012 was
noted for a rejection of biblical values on a massive scale. For the first time in our nation's history, a clear majority of Americans came out to
end the biblical definition of marriage, as did the

president. That's just one example. The downward slide of America has accelerated this past year at an alarming rate. All of the symptoms of the darkness spreading are indications of a much bigger problem: *America is turning away from God, and with increasing rapidity.*[1]

We must remember the words of Thomas Jefferson, which are inscribed on the interior wall of the Jefferson Memorial:

> God who gave us life gave us liberty. Can the liberties of a nation be secure when we have removed a conviction that these liberties are the gift of God? Indeed I tremble for my country when I reflect that God is just, that his justice cannot sleep forever. Commerce between master and slave is despotism. Nothing is more certainly written in the book of fate than that these people are to be free. Establish a law for educating the common people. This it is the business of the state and on a general plan.
>
> —THOMAS JEFFERSON

Today, America is removing God from every part of this once-blessed nation. We rose to become the world's most powerful nation, both politically and economically. Yet our rise to success and prosperity has now led us to self-sufficiency and a turning away from God. Yes, we too have forgotten God.

Where will the church in America be in ten years? Here's what Jonathan Cahn says:

> We have two choices before us. Either the Church will become more radical; more pure; more bold;

more uncompromising; more counter-cultural—leading America to revival. Or it will become worthless; without salt; compromised; confused; embracing of darkness and the world.[2]

Pastor Cahn sees the gray area disappearing: "Darkness is getting darker. Sins that used to be hidden are now becoming increasingly blatant and celebrated. There is a polarization taking place."[3] But he also believes that along with the darkness is hope: "The light is also getting lighter. Persecution is coming to the Church, but from that will emerge a Church that once again lives boldly; a Church that changes the world. Christians often talk about the Church during the book of Acts. That church had no gray areas."[4] That is the church Jonathan Cahn believes awaits America—if God's people will heed God's warnings.

The Future of America

Cahn also believes the heartfelt message of Luke 12:48: "From everyone who has been given much, much will be required." As a nation, we have become so arrogant in our blessings, we've forgotten from Whom all blessings flow. But our hope lies in our response to the warnings—a hope found in God's Word:

> [If] My people who are called by My name humble themselves and pray and seek My face and turn from their wicked ways, then I will hear from heaven, will forgive their sin and will heal their land.
>
> —2 CHRONICLES 7:14

In 722 BC the capital of the northern kingdom, Samaria, was destroyed, and its inhabitants were removed, just as the prophet Isaiah foretold. As a result of their defiance, its people would disappear among the nations. They would be known as "the lost tribes of Israel." In the words of Ginny Dent Brench, we must ask: "What will happen to America? The Bible does not say. Cahn has written *The Harbinger* in the hope that America will wake up before it's too late. His evidence is compelling and Biblical. It's evidence that demands a response."[5]

The Harbinger and Jonathan Cahn

Jonathan Cahn wasn't seeking to bring a prophetic message to America. After 9/11, as he was praying, he was led to a particular section of Scripture in Isaiah concerning the first warning of judgment given to Israel. This scripture, Isaiah 9:10, would become the "decoder" verse of *The Harbinger*.

Later, as he stood at the corner of Ground Zero, his attention was drawn to an object. Something said, "Seek it out." He began searching the Scriptures, and the mystery began to unfold. It was the first puzzle piece of the ancient mystery that kept getting bigger and bigger, deeper and deeper until he was completely blown away. It was an ancient mystery that lay behind everything from 9/11 to everything that happened after. It was so specific that it even foretold the precise actions and words of American leaders. It was mind-boggling.

When Cahn shared the revelations with his congregation at the Jerusalem Center/Beth Israel, they were likewise blown away. Everyone felt it was a word from the Lord that had to go forth to the nation. As he began working on the book, an entire second stream of mysteries began to unfold—ancient mysteries that lay behind the collapse of the American nation, mysteries so specific that they pinpointed events down to the days and hours.

When Cahn began to write the book in the form in which it now exists, that of a prophet revealing the mystery through a series of seals, the words just flowed out as if the book was already written before he wrote it.[6]

How *The Harbinger* Is Impacting Lives

The Harbinger has impacted the lives of many who have been gripped by the uncanny scriptural parallels of Isaiah 9:10 and what's happening in current events since 9/11. The message is for believer and unbeliever alike, a call to salvation, repentance, and revival. It is a critical message, a life-changing message, and perhaps one of the most important messages ever published.

The following testimonials reflect the experience of the thousands of people whose lives have been changed forever by this message:

> If you doubt [God] being in control—or if you doubt the parallels between God's dealings with ancient Israel and the events in America since and including 9/11, reading *The Harbinger* with an open mind will change that. Reading it with an open heart might just change your life.

What a riveting book! Once I started reading, I truly didn't want to stop....The story, as it unfolded, completely captivated my attention.

The Harbinger by Jonathan Cahn was written for a time such as this, mesmerizing and fascinating from beginning to end. In light of current events, this book is an eye opener for every American....This book surely is a wake-up call for Americans to get on their knees and reclaim this great nation before it's too late.

The Harbinger opened my eyes to the dangerous path America is walking in light of the parallels shown in scripture. I couldn't put it down. *The Harbinger* is a MUST read for all who love America and want to see it prevail as a blessed nation.

After 9/11, America should have been saying, "America bless God," not "God bless America."...Let repentance start with me, and thanks to Rabbi Cahn for this sober reminder.

It took me to a new level of faith in the God of the Bible and the fact that He still speaks prophetically today because He is not only a God who judges, but a God who loves—a love so deep that He would go to such lengths to give so many warnings to a nation that has turned so far from Him.

Once I started reading, I couldn't stop or put it down. Why are these things happening to our beloved nation? Simply because we've turned our back on God and now He is judging us....Unless we turn back to His Face and His Truth, this country will cease to be a place where freedom reigns. God help us!

If you only read one book this year this should be it....This message must be urgently shouted from the rooftop to anyone who cares about America's future.

If you are a total agnostic or atheist, this is just an interesting book, but NO ONE can deny there are way too many mere coincidences in this story to be coincidences....God is not one of our hopes—He is our ONLY hope.

I could not put this down, read it in two hours. Seeing our own recent history matched up with Biblical prophecy is unnerving to say the least, but it is what so many need to hear. I can tell you I will make personal changes in my own life because of this book....If we are to save our country it will start with each of us looking in the mirror and saying, "I will make a change. It starts with me!"

I am going to begin to pray over this work every day; we must turn back to God or face the judgment of God. I feel sorry for people who can't open their minds to entertain the idea that there is a just and holy God in charge of everything. They will spend an eternity wishing they had!

It is not only that people across the nation and world have been amazed by the revelations in *The Harbinger,* but also that those revelations have proven life-changing:

What I loved most about *The Harbinger* is that it is a vivid reminder that there are NO coincidences...ever! I got a glimpse of the LORD as the Word of God paints Him—high, exalted and absolutely sovereign! I've always been amazed by

God's sovereignty and I was very blessed to have Bible teachers that taught me, very accurately, of this attribute of God. Jehovah Sabaoth (i.e. the LORD of hosts) has always been my favorite name of God because it speaks of His majestic sovereignty! I knew instantly that Jonathan Cahn is a man who has an exalted view of God, just as I do, and God's glory came shining through in his book. I felt we were kindred spirits right off the bat…but I guess that's because we both have the same Spirit living in us!

I took the *repentance challenge* in the book seriously and began to do some introspection—asking God to show me if there be a wicked way in *me* and wanting Him to purge that from me because I did not want to be a part of the problem. Little did I know what God had in store for me. God was about to take me on the journey of a lifetime and lead me to places I never dreamed I would go in answer to my prayer.

May it be known that I owe Jonathan Cahn a great debt, which is probably why I'm such a staunch defender of his. He caused me to look deep within myself and I realized I needed to repent of some Phariseeism of my own, and, once I did, my understanding exploded!

This, in a nutshell, is my own personal testimony as to how *The Harbinger* and Jonathan Cahn were the vessels God used to transform my life in recent days, and I am forever grateful to God for His tender mercy in granting me repentance! I say, God bless Jonathan Cahn for his patience and faithfulness.[7]

—Laura

Once in a great while something comes along and shakes you to your core.

That happened to me recently in the form of the written word: *The Harbinger*, a book I received as a Christmas gift from my daughter and son-in-law.

Little did I know that this would be a new beginning for this old man. Having been a Christian for years, although "backslidden" as they say, I was going about my merry way until I was awakened by an internal alarm. The voice of a prophet no less, speaking to me as clearly as if we were face to face, telling me of danger from the past, the present and the future.

This story of an ancient mystery that holds the secret of America's future is interwoven into a fictional host of characters that is spellbinding and so real that you are left breathless and frightened with a renewed since of urgency to tell the world their need to turn back to God before it is too late.

No matter what you believe, or who you believe in, I implore you to read or have someone read this book to you. It will impact your life.[8]

—FREDERICK

The Harbinger

As of this writing, *The Harbinger* is still on the nation's best seller-list and has been there longer than most best sellers. It has been translated into Spanish, French, and Portuguese, and it is being translated into German, Norwegian, Hungarian, and Swedish. Its sales trajectory puts it into the category of only three other books of faith in the last quarter-century. The message of *The Harbinger* continues to go forth with no sign of slowing down. It is being read by Jews and Gentiles, Catholics and Protestants, Baptists and charismatics, Mormons, atheists, pastors, housewives, university professors, senators, representatives, presidential candidates, and the most powerful of national leaders.

And all this from a man who was not looking for a message, who never before wrote a book, and who, when he wrote it, did so at a rapid-fire pace. *The Harbinger* has become a phenomenon.

The Harbinger was unlikely in its origin, in its execution, in its publication, in its spread, and in its record-breaking success. But so were the prophetic messages of revelation and warning brought forth to ancient Israel in the days before its destruction. And such messages were always—always—the subject of controversy and attack. *The Harbinger* is thus in very good company.

The question must be asked: If God were to send forth a prophetic word of warning to America, what would it sound like? Multitudes would answer: It would sound very much like *The Harbinger*.

We Have Forgotten God

The church in America has failed to be salt and light to the people of this nation. Salt preserves, and light cuts through the darkness. They're both radical. They're change agents. Salt prevents decay. Light eliminates darkness. They dramatically change everything they come into contact with. But Jonathan Cahn believes the church in America is failing to be both:

If the church were being "salt" and "light", the
condition of the nation would be very different.
It would not be decaying and rotting at the rate
it is; the darkness would not be spreading.[9]

Without any doubt whatsoever, *The Harbinger*
has helped many people understand the incom-
prehensible kaleidoscope of events that were triggered by these harbingers—events that no one
could have planned, contrived, or had any control
over.

We were mere spectators up until now of these
events—and witnesses who, having read this mag-
nificent little book, now stand ready to call upon
our God for this nation, to take up the call to
warn others throughout the land, to act as the
prophet Elijah did in his day and John the Baptist
did in his day in the spirit and power of that great
prophet of old, to prepare a highway for our God
and the coming of the Messiah, the Lord Jesus, as
we witness all of these things come to pass before
our eyes.

But there are many who have yet to rise up in
action to join with those in God's family who are
fighting for the return of the godly foundation
of our nation. The church must once again seek
God's approval over man's. It must become radical
for God—bolder, uncompromising. These are like
the days of Elijah, of Jeremiah, of Isaiah. Those
men weren't popular, but they refused to soften
the message. The church must draw a line in the
sand—to take a stand. If we are going to make a
difference, we must become more different.

I conclude this book with the challenge Jonathan Cahn presented to the nation at the 2013 Presidential Inaugural Prayer Breakfast:

The time is late. The hour is critical. A great nation proceeds in rapid spiritual descent. And the signs of warning and judgment are manifesting in the land. The shadow of judgment is upon us. And for those who would be ask, "How, in light of judgment, can one be saved, or safe?", we give this answer—the word in Hebrew for safety and salvation is Yeshua. Yeshua is the name which we know in English as "Jesus." Outside of Him there is no safety. But inside of Him there is no fear. It was for Him and in His name that this nation, this civilization, this city on a hill, named America, came into existence. And it is only to Him and in His name that its problems can ultimately be answered. He remains the answer, the light in the darkness, and the hope when all other hopes are faded and gone. And to all who come, He will receive. And He calls out, "Come."

For all you who dwell in darkness, it's time to come. And you will not be turned away.

And for all you who know Him, for you His people, it is time to put away any shade of darkness and compromise—and take up the mantle of your calling.

It's time to be the salt of the earth and the light of the world you were called to be, in truth, in power, and love. It is time to light up the darkness.

It's time to be strong. It's time to be bold. It's time to be radical.

The watchmen are crying out, and the trumpets are sounding.

And the voice of the Lord is calling to this nation and saying, "Return."

And calling to His people and saying, "Return."

Let the word go forth. Let the power of God be seen in this land. And let revival burst forth like a mighty river.

The voice of one crying in the wilderness:
Prepare the way of the Lord.
Prepare the way of the Lord.
Make straight in the wilderness a highway for
   our God
Every valley shall be exalted,
And every mountain and hill shall be cast down
The crooked way shall be made straight
And the rough way shall become a plain
And the glory of the Lord shall be revealed
And all flesh will see it together
For the mouth of the Lord has spoken…
Arise and shine for your light has come
And the glory of the Lord has risen upon you
And nations will come to your light
And kings to the brightness of your rising.

In the name above all names that are named,
Yeshua Ha Mashiach, Jesus the Messiah
The King of kings
And the Lord of lords
The Light of the World
The Hope of America
The Lion of the Tribe of Judah
And the glory of His people Israel
AMEN & AMEN.[10]

Notes

1—The Phenomenon of *The Harbinger*

1. Terry James, "*The Harbinger* by Jonathan Cahn: A Book Review by Terry James," *Rapture Ready* (blog), http://www.raptureready.com/terry/book11.html (accessed June 30, 2013). Used by permission.

2. Rabbi Jonathan Cahn, address at the Presidential Inaugural Prayer Breakfast held in Washington DC, Monday, January 21, 2013.

3. Ibid.

2—The Mystery, the Message, and the Warning

1. Dawson Elliott, "America's Future Seen Through 'The Harbinger'—by Jonathan Cahn: Was 9/11 a Warning From God?", *Expanding Your World* (blog), September 30, 2012, http://www.expandingyourworld.com/americas-future-seen-through-the-harbinger-by-jonathan-cahn-was-911-a-warning-from-god (accessed June 28, 2013).

2. AncientReplicas.com, "Assyrian King Blinding Prisoners," http://www.ancientreplicas.com/assyrian-blinding.html (accessed June 28, 2013).

3. Governor George E. Pataki's remarks at the laying of the cornerstone for the Freedom Tower, July 4, 2004, http://www.renewnyc.com/content/speeches/Gov_speech_Freedom_Tower.pdf (accessed June 28, 2013).

4. This was the first act of the US government: "The gathering would be recorded in the Annals of Congress as part of the first-ever joint session of Congress with an acting president. The inauguration of the United States, as we know it, began with a sacred gathering before God" (Jonathan Cahn, *The Harbinger* [Lake Mary, FL: FrontLine, 2011], 202–203).

5. One of the favorite bumper stickers seen on many car bumpers throughout the nation in the aftermath of September 11 was one that contained the colors of the American flag with a caption that read, "The Power of Pride." I recalled that I too felt a sense of defiance inside to rebuild the towers as they were, but taller and stronger. This is how the nation and its leaders felt in the following months. Our pride had been wounded.

6. Senator John Edwards, remarks given at the Congressional Black Caucus Prayer Breakfast, September 11, 2004, as quoted by the American Presidency Project, http://www.presidency.ucsb.edu/ws/?pid=84922 (accessed June 28, 2013).

7. U.S. Senate Majority Leader Tom Daschle, remarks made to a joint session of Congress, September 12, 2001, as excerpted by Eric Brown, "'We Will Rebuild…,'" *Tomorrow's World* (blog), http://www.tomorrowsworld.org/node/5703 (accessed June 28, 2013).

8. "The attempt of a nation to defy the course of its judgment, apart from repentance, will, instead, set in motion a chain of events to bring about the very calamity it sought to avert" (Cahn, *The Harbinger*, 141).

9. These two tribes were descendants of Joseph's two sons. Manasseh was a half-tribe; this term only designated a small part of the tribe. The territory to the west of the Jordan River was given to the tribes of Gad and Reuben and half of the tribe of Manasseh. The other half of the tribe was located on the other side of the Jordan River.

10. The Rev. Dr. Daniel Matthews, rector of Trinity Church, remarks given at the dedication of the Tree of Hope, November 2003.

11. The Hebrew word for "release."

12. WhiteHouse.gov, "Remarks of President Barack Obama—as Prepared for Delivery, Address to Joint Session of Congress, Tuesday, February 24, 2009," http://www.whitehouse.gov/the_press_office/Remarks-of-President-Barack-Obama-Address-to-Joint-Session-of-Congress/ (accessed June 28, 2013).

13. Cahn, *The Harbinger*, 207–208.

14. Jonathan Cahn, "The Message to America," remarks given at the Presidential Inaugural Prayer Breakfast, January 21, 2013, https://www.facebook.com/notes/the-harbinger-jonathan-cahn-official-site/the-following-is-the-transcript-of-the-key-note-address-jonathan-gave-at-the-pre/456242577776032 (accessed June 28, 2013).

15. Ibid.

16. Cahn, *The Harbinger*, 239.

17. Jonathan Cahn, *The Harbinger Companion With Study Guide* (Lake Mary, FL: Charisma, 2013), 170.

3—The Harbingers: Alive and Well (Part 1)

1. See Jeremiah 19.

4—The Harbingers: Alive and Well (Part 2)

1. Cahn, *The Harbinger*, 118–119.

5—Other Mysteries of *The Harbinger* Explained

1. Cahn, *The Harbinger*, 49.
2. *Faith's Corner* (blog), "Comment Posted on *The Harbinger*," June 30, 2012, http:// watchpraystand.blogspot.com/2012/06/comment -posted-on-harbinger.html (accessed June 29, 2013).

6—The Meaning of the Word

1. Hermeneutics is defined as the science and method of biblical interpretation.
2. Charles Swindoll, "Samuel: The Boy Who Heard God's Voice," sermon preached September 11, 2012.
3. Literally, "God-breathed."

7—The Isaiah 9:10 Connection

1. Joey Faust, as quoted by *The Pepster's Post*, "A Reply and Clarification to KJOS Ministries on *The Harbinger*," March 9, 2013, http:// avoiceincyberspace.blogspot.com/2013/03/a-reply -clarification-to-kjos.html (accessed June 28, 2013).
2. Ephraim, the northern kingdom, with its capital in Samaria.
3. Judah and Benjamin, the southern kingdom, with its capital in Jerusalem.
4. Modern-day Er Ram.

5. From Ephraim and Manasseh, sons of Joseph, Rachel's son (Gen. 30:22–24; 48:1–2).

6. Joshua 18:11.

8—Prophecy, Pattern, or Coincidence?

1. The Port Authority of New York and New Jersey, "1,776-Foot Freedom Tower Will Be World's Tallest Building, Reclaim New York's Skyline," press release, July 4, 2004, http://www.panynj.gov/press-room/press-item.cfm?headLine_id=489 (accessed June 28, 2013).

2. Cahn, *The Harbinger Companion With Study Guide*, 88.

3. Alexandra Twin, "Stocks Crushed," CNNMoney.com, http://money.cnn.com/2008/09/29/markets/markets_newyork/ (accessed July 22, 2013).

4. Nancy Trejos, "Retirement Savings Lose $2 Trillion in 15 Months," *Washington Post*, October 8, 2008, http://articles.washingtonpost.com/2008-10-08/politics/36857294_1_assets-decline-defined-contribution-plans-retirement-plans (accessed July 22, 2013).

5. This quote from an observant Jewish commenter named Rachel is found at *The Pepster's Post*, March 9, 2013.

6. See also 2 Chronicles 32:31 and Isaiah 39, both related to this incident.

7. Though there are differences between modern and ancient Hebrew.

9—The Truth About America's Founding

1. Encyclopedia Virginia, "First Charter of Virginia (1606)," transcription from original, http://www.encyclopediavirginia.org/First_Charter_of_Virginia_1606 (accessed June 28, 2013).

2. VirginiaPlaces.org, "Boundaries and Charters of Virginia," http://www.virginiaplaces.org/boundaries/charters.html (accessed June 28, 2013).

3. The Rail Splitter, "Richard Hakluyt, Reasons for Colonization, 1585," wikispace document, http://therailsplitter.wikispaces.com/file/view/Ch.+2+Hakluyt+and+Frethorne.pdf (accessed June 28, 2013).

4. "Hunt had been vicar of Reculver, Kent, but was forced to leave his wife and two children in disgrace, in 1602, owing to his wife's adulterous 'seeing too much of one John Taylor.' In 1606, he was forced to leave his second parish, at Old Heathfield in Sussex, when he was accused of having his own adulterous affair with his servant, Thomasina Plumber, as well as 'absenteeism, and neglecting of his congregation'" (Wikipedia, "Robert Hunt [Chaplain]," http://en.wikipedia.org/wiki/Robert_Hunt_(chaplain), citing Jocelyn Wingfield, *Virginia's True Founder* [2007], 163; W. C. Renshaw, *Notes From the Act Books of the Archdeaconry Court of Lewes in Sussex Archaeological Collections*, vol. 49 [Bancroft, 1906]; and Benjamin Woolley, *Savage Kingdom* [2007], 36).

5. As quoted by Ministers-Best-Friend.com, "George Washington Prays, God Sends

Supernatural Fog to Allow Escape," http://www
.ministers-best-friend.com/George-Washington
-Prays-God-sends-Supernatural-Fog-to-Allow
-Escape.html (accessed June 28, 2013).

6. Ibid.

7. Ibid.

8. Ibid.

9. Ibid.

10. Historic Valley Forge, "Washington's Earnest
Prayer," http://www.ushistory.org/valleyforge/
washington/earnestprayer.html (accessed June 28,
2013).

11. William J. Johnson, *George Washington,
The Christian* (New York: The Abingdon Press,
1919).

12. Frank Ceresi and Carol McMains, "The
George Washington Inaugural Bible," FC Associates, http://www.fcassociates.com/ntbible.htm
(accessed June 28, 2013).

13. Ibid.

14. National Archives and Records Administration, transcription of "Washington's Inaugural
Address of 1789," April 30, 1789, http://www
.archives.gov/exhibits/american_originals/inaugtxt
.html (accessed June 28, 2013).

15. Written at Newburg, June 8, 1783, and sent
to the governors of all the states. Published in
the Army and Navy Hymnal, 1942.

16. Cahn, *The Harbinger*, 204–208.

17. Jacob Prasch, from a video titled, "Interview with Jacob Prasch Understanding End Time,"
Moriel Ministries.

18. As America has blessed the Jewish people and been a haven for them, so God has blessed America; and as the United States supported and aided the fledgling state of Israel, so has God blessed this nation. (See Genesis 12:2.)

10—Israel and America: Unique Among Nations

1. Ishmael became the father of twelve princes, comprising the Arabs (Gen. 17:20).
2. Prasch, "Interview with Jacob Prasch Understanding End Time."
3. Cubans are not classified as refugees because they are an exiled people. They do not consider themselves refugees because they have come here for political and not economic reasons.

11—The True America-Israel Connection

1. God spares nothing to save His creation.
2. The only promise that is exclusive to the Jewish people is the promise of the land God gave to Abraham, Isaac, and Jacob.
3. Excerpts from "What Really Ails America," condensed from a speech by William J. Bennett, delivered December 7, 1993, at the Heritage Foundation, Washington DC, reprinted in *Reader's Digest*, April 1994.
4. Ibid.
5. Ibid.

12—Mysticism, Dreams, Kabbalah, and the Enlightenment

1. Cahn, *The Harbinger*, 252.

2. Some of the material in the previous sections on mysticism and Kabbalah were excerpted from Jonathan Cahn's responses to an interview conducted by Mike LeMay and Amy Spreeman, "Harbinger Author Jonathan Cahn Answers Questions," *Stand Up for the Truth!* (blog), http://standupforthetruth.com/2012/06/harbinger-author-johnathan-cahn-answers-questions (accessed June 28, 2013).

3. Years later, Abraham and Sarah's son, Isaac, would pull the same stunt on Abimelech, but Abimelech would discover Isaac and Rebekah to be married and would confront Isaac about it. Abimelech made it a capital offense if anyone was caught touching Rebekah (Gen. 26:6–11).

13—The Importance of Good Discernment

1. Jonathan Cahn, "The End of Biblical Discernment? (Perhaps in This Case)," *Rapture Ready* (blog), http://www.raptureready.com/soap/cahn3.html (accessed June 28, 2013).

2. Cahn, *The Harbinger*, 251.

14—Does *The Harbinger* Add to Scripture?

1. Jude 9; the words "when he disputed with the devil and argued about the body of Moses" are found in the early extrabiblical text the Ascension of Moses, also called the Assumption of Moses.

2. Dr. Harold Lindsell, "Introduction to the Letter of Jude," in *The Harper Study Bible*, New American Standard Bible (Grand Rapids, MI: Zondervan Publishing Company, 1985).

3. Cited in Joshua 10:13 and 2 Samuel 1:18.

4. See Numbers 21:14.

5. See 1 Kings 8:12–13 (Septuagint).

6. Cited in 1 Kings 14:19, 29. This book is again mentioned in 1 Kings 16:20 regarding King Zimri, and throughout 1 and 2 Kings.

7. See 2 Chronicles 9:29; 12:15; 13:22. Iddo was a seer who lived during the reigns of Solomon, Rehoboam, and Abijah.

8. See 1 Samuel 10:25.

9. Cited in 1 Kings 11:41.

10. See 1 Chronicles 27:24.

11. See 1 Chronicles 29:29.

12. See 1 Chronicles 29:29; 2 Chronicles 9:29.

13. See 1 Chronicles 29:29.

14. See 1 Kings 14:2–18. Also cited in 2 Chronicles 9:29.

15. Cited in 2 Chronicles 16:11; 27:7; 32:32.

16. Cited in 2 Chronicles 20:34.

17. Cited in 2 Chronicles 24:27.

18. See 2 Chronicles 26:22.

19. Cited in 2 Chronicles 32:32.

20. See 2 Chronicles 33:18; also called the Acts and Prayers of Manasseh.

21. See 2 Chronicles 33:19.

22. See 2 Chronicles 35:25.

23. See Esther 2:23; 6:1; 10:2; Nehemiah 12:23.

24. Claudius was Roman emperor from AD 41–54.

25. The reason we know of the famine is because extrabiblical sources have recorded the history of it having taken place exactly as prophesied and that the nature of it was a famine.

26. It is this life that releases us from the power of sin and death and empowers every Christian to live consecrated for the Lord.

27. A requirement of those who held the office of apostle was that they were eyewitnesses of Jesus' teachings and works and of His resurrection.

15—Does *The Harbinger* Preach the Gospel?

1. Cahn, *The Harbinger*, 226.
2. Ibid., 226–227.
3. Ibid., 228.
4. Proverbs 21:2.
5. Cahn, *The Harbinger*, 228–230.
6. Ibid., 230–235.
7. Jonathan Cahn, as quoted in Dawson Elliott, "America's Future Seen Through 'The Harbinger'—by Jonathan Cahn: Was 9/11 a Warning From God?"
8. Ibid.

16—Promoting *The Harbinger* Promotes the Gospel

1. National Archives and Records Administration, "Washington's Inaugural Address of 1789."
2. This section was adapted from Cahn, "The Message to America."
3. *Orthopraxy* means, "correct behavior"; *orthodoxy* means, "correct belief." I use the term Christian orthopraxy, which is "faith in action and practice," to differentiate from its use in Judaism, which refers to a Torah lifestyle and adherence to rabbinic halaka.

4. Dwight Douville, "An Open Response to the Berean Call's Recent Article by Mark Dinsmore," *The Things to Come* (blog), August 8, 2012, http://thethings2come.org/?p=740 (accessed June 29, 2013). Used by permission.

5. Terry James, "*The Harbinger*'s Bottom Line," *Rapture Ready* (blog), http://www.raptureready .com/rr-the-harbinger.html (accessed June 29, 2013). Used by permission.

17—What's Next?

1. This paragraph was adapted from an interview with Jonathan Cahn by David Jesse, "Solutions: Jonathan Cahn, Author of *The Harbinger*," *Third Option Men* (blog), http://www.thirdoptionmen .org/blog/solutions-jonathan-cahn-author -harbinger/ (accessed June 29, 2013).

2. Ibid.

3. Ibid.

4. Ibid.

5. Ginny Dent Brant, "Jonathan Cahn Interview Part II: The Harbingers on American Soil," *Sonoma Christian Home* (blog), June 5, 2013, http://sonomachristianhome.com/2013/06/ jonathan-cahn-interview-part-ii-the-harbingers-on -american-soil/ (accessed June 29, 2013).

6. David W. Thornton, "Interview with Jonathan Cahn, Author of 'The Harbinger' (Photos)," Examiner.com, January 21, 2013, http://www .examiner.com/article/interview-with-jonathan -cahn-author-of-the-harbinger (accessed June 29, 2013).

7. From an e-mail I received from Laura, affectionately known as "Ladybug." Used with permission.

8. TriCities.com, "Read 'The Harbinger'; It Will Change Your Life," letter to the editor, February 20, 2013, http://www.tricities.com/news/opinion_columns/article_18e80716-7b14-11e2-af68 -0019bb30f31a.html (accessed June 29, 2013). Used with permission.

9. Jonathan Cahn, as quoted by Jesse, "Solutions: Jonathan Cahn, Author of *The Harbinger*."

10. Jonathan Cahn, "The Message to America."